HOUSE OF
FLOWERS

ASHLEE JANE

HOUSE OF
FLOWERS

30 floristry projects to bring
the magic of flowers into your home

greenfinch

CONTENTS

PROJECT FINDER

INTRODUCTION

It's fair to say that The Suffolk Nest wasn't exactly part of the plan. While I'd always had a passion for flowers, and our home was often full to bursting with blooms, my professional life was rooted in my corporate sales role. I loved my job, but a part of me yearned to lean into my creativity.

The opportunity arose in 2014 when a friend invited me to a Christmas wreath-making class. But to be honest, when the day came, I didn't want to go. I'd had a long day of driving for work and could barely stand the idea of jumping back in the car. I pushed through my reservations for the sake of my friends, and it was one of the best decisions I've ever made.

That wreath-making class sparked something inside of me that changed everything! I was captivated by the craft, the fragrant foliage, and the stunning finished piece that I'd made. The class reignited my imagination and I soon began creating bouquets, flower crowns and home arrangements while immersing myself in the world of flower arranging to learn as much as I possibly could.

My renewed interest in flower arranging coincided with the launch of my interiors Instagram account. Decorating my home has long been an outlet for my creative streak and I loved sharing my designs and projects online in the hope of inspiring others. When my floral work started to feature on the account, the response was overwhelming. In fact, I received so many lovely comments and messages that I started to share more floristry content, from tips and how-to guides to video-styling workshops.

When Covid-19 hit and we went into lockdown, I was on maternity leave from work. The enforced isolation and time spent indoors highlighted the impact that fresh flowers can have in the home. They bring life, beauty and joy, while also marking the seasons and allowing us to embrace transitional styles without needing to redecorate every three months! During this time,

I found comfort in creating seasonal arrangements and getting the whole family involved. We used our daily walks to forage for foliage alongside more unusual elements, finding blackberry brambles in autumn, fresh rosemary in summer, and discarded feathers in spring.

Christmas has also taken on a new meaning thanks to wreath-making. Not only did a festive class act as a catalyst for me to eventually run The Suffolk Nest fulltime, but our 2020 holiday wreath kits made it all possible. I designed the kits to replace our cancelled workshops during the pandemic and expected to sell no more than 50 in total. But the reaction was incredible and, despite several logistical challenges, we were able to send seasonal cheer to hundreds of people at a tough time. Our kits brought people together at a time when many of us were forcibly separated from our loved ones and local communities. It was an incredible feeling and we felt like we'd created something very special.

Now, eight years on from that evening class, The Suffolk Nest has blossomed into a business that I'm incredibly proud of. We have a reach of over 300k followers worldwide, I deliver free weekly tutorials every week, work closely with mental health charities, and sell a range of items from seasonal wreath kits and faux flowers to fresh flower stems and arrangements.

My mission is to make flowers accessible to everyone. I hope this book will serve to nurture your creativity, capture your imagination, and encourage you to explore the magical ways that flowers can transform your home year-round.

Ashlee Jane

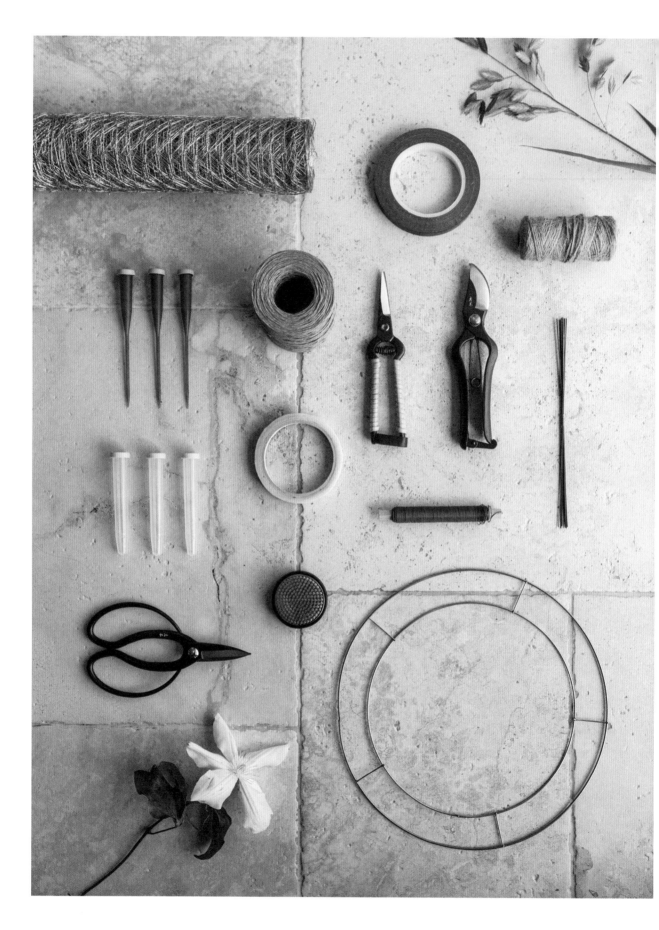

FLORISTRY BASICS

Tools

There is an abundance of tools and materials available to help make floristry easier. However, it can feel a little overwhelming and complex at first. I remember standing in our local sundry supplier's warehouse gazing at all the different tools and wondering what on earth I would ever use them for. Over the years, I have come to realise that I only need a few good tools in my kit to create the designs I love, so I am sharing what I consider to be the best and most essential tools here.

FLORISTRY SCISSORS & SECATEURS
If you invest in just one item from this tool kit, it needs to be a good pair of scissors that are only used for your flowers. There are many on the market, but my favourites are Niwaki Higurashi Scissors and Niwaki Sentei Secateurs. I use the scissors on a daily basis and their carbon steel blade helps to reduce bacteria build-up and rust, and I use the secateurs for stronger, woody branches such as blossom, viburnum and lilac for a clean, sharp cut. It's important to take care of your tools so that they last longer and remain effective. Simply scrape away any resin from the blades. If necessary, rinse with water; you can also use a little washing-up liquid and a gentle scrubbing brush. Ensure you dry your tools thoroughly to prevent rust. And there are bonus points for wiping the blades with a drop of camellia oil after use and not using your best floristry scissors for cutting chicken and reel wire.

FABRIC SCISSORS
It's a good idea to have a pair of scissors solely for fabric cutting so you can get a nice clean cut on any ribbons you want to use in your designs. I have a small yellow pair so I can easily identify them from my others.

BUCKETS
When allowing your flowers to drink and rest during the initial conditioning

stage, it's a good idea to have some big buckets to hand to place them in. Over the years I have collected a number of Dutch floristry buckets that you can often find listed for sale on online marketplaces, but they can be pricey. They're ideal if you feel floristry is something you'd like to take a little more seriously than just a side hobby, but otherwise I recommend powder-coated steel floristry buckets, available in small, medium and large sizes to cater for a wide variety of stem lengths. Alternatively, you could use some large apothecary-style glass vases that have medium-sized openings to ensure your flowers have plenty of room to breathe and develop.

COMPOST BAG

When I started experimenting with flowers, I was far too engrossed in the design to care much about the mess I was creating – but my goodness I created a huge mess and I would need to spend a lot of time cleaning up after! Standard household bins are often too small for long flower stems and they will snag the bin bags. I recommend getting a collapsible fabric compost bag that you can easily transport from place to place and tidy as you go.

Mechanics

The term 'mechanics' refers to the materials used to help create a support and structure for your designs – they are your secret weapons to creating truly breath-taking designs.

TWINE

Mostly used for binding hand-tied bouquets, available in both natural and green colour options from most hardware stores and garden centres.

PAPER-COVERED WIRE

This is the best option for binding that requires extra support and security, such as for large bouquets or garlands. I particularly like how neatly it secures without the need for unsightly knots or bows.

REEL WIRE

Available in green, black and silver either on a small wooden stick or plastic reel. I mainly use this for wreath-making as it's ideal for binding the flowers and foliage onto wreath bases.

STEMTEX

Mostly used for wired designs, such as the Midsummer Crown on page 110. It is self-adhesive and activated by stretch and warmth. It can take a little getting used to at first, but it's brilliant as it helps to lock moisture into the stems.

POT TAPE

Also known as anchor tape, this strong waterproof tape is available in dark green and clear and I mostly use it to secure chicken wire within vases. I find the dark green to be much more effective so only use the clear tape for light-coloured or glass vases where the tape may be on show.

CHICKEN WIRE

I use classic galvanised (to prevent rust) chicken wire available from most hardware stores or garden centres. The size I use most is a 2.5cm (1in) gap between the hexagons and I use a higher-end gauge (20) that suits both small and larger arrangements for additional support. You can also find specific floristry mesh and plasticised chicken wire, which is often green and waterproof.

KENZAN/FLOWER FROG

These originate from Japan where they were used to create ikebana arrangements – a contemporary floral design in low shallow bowls. They are weighted discs with metal spikes that you insert the stems into for strong support. I secure them down at the bottom of a low bowl with a little floral fix, and chicken wire for an additional support higher up to create beautifully light and airy designs.

FLORAL FIX/PUTTY

This is a handy one to have in your tool kit to secure kenzans/ flower frogs into position and prevent them from moving in your vase.

FLORISTRY WIRE

Available in a huge and slightly overwhelming range of thicknesses and lengths. I favour more natural methods, but floristry wire does have a place; for example, I find it an ideal base for making flower crowns, so long as you choose a sturdy thickness that will hold the flowers in place securely.

WATER VIALS & FLOWER PICKS

Slim plastic tubes with rubber caps available with or without extended spikes (known as flower picks). I use these most often for wreaths, where the damp moss isn't going to provide quite enough hydration for a particular flower; I simply poke the spike into the moss, cut away the excess and top up the tube with water as required. You can reuse these as many times as you wish.

WIRE WREATH FRAME

Provides a perfect base for moss-based wreaths and can be used over and over again. I usually use a 30cm (12in) frame as this creates an abundant, full-sized wreath for a front door.

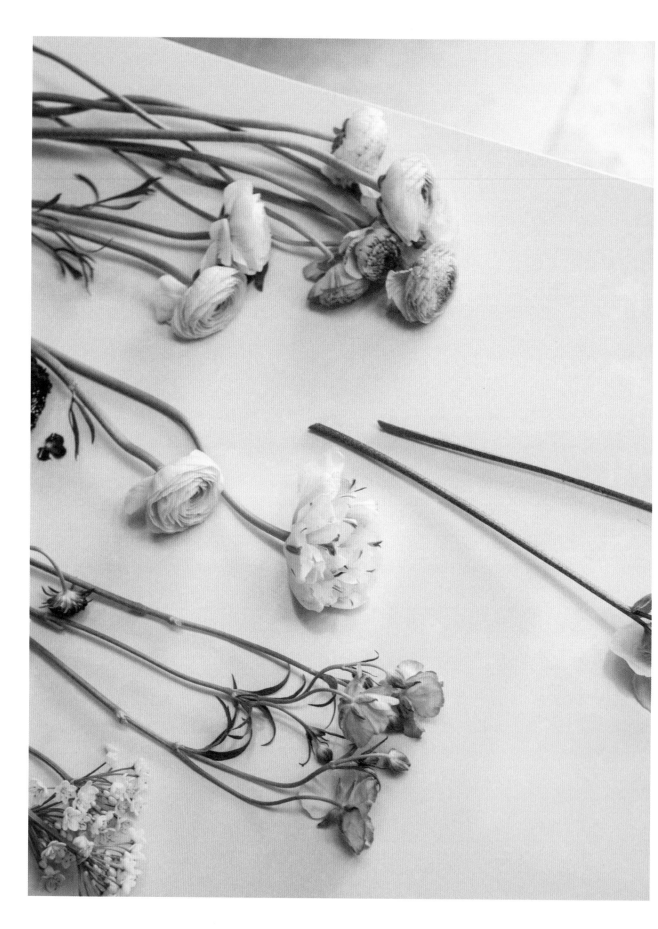

WHERE TO SOURCE YOUR FLOWERS

In the early days of my flower journey when I was experimenting with different techniques, I only used our small garden, local markets, supermarkets and florists to source flowers, and initially this was enough. However, after securing my first wedding client, I realised that I would have to find other sources for flowers as it wasn't cost effective to buy what I needed from local florists, and markets and supermarkets couldn't offer the range necessary. So I set about searching for different sources. Since then, I have spent years building long-standing relationships with suppliers and growers whom I trust and rely on to provide the flowers I need. In this section, I share the different options that are available for sourcing flowers, whether you are looking to start a floristry business, or you simply just enjoy arranging flowers.

Wholesalers

ONLINE WHOLESALERS

These are ideal for professional florists as these companies can offer good prices and a wide range, but you'll need a registered business in order to create an account. These companies buy their flowers at huge auction platforms from all over the world and sell them on to florists. Due to the perishable nature of flowers, knowing when you need to order flowers for the correct delivery date is crucial. Once you have set up an account with an online wholesaler, a representative should talk this through with you. You select your flowers from an online platform where there is usually a time limit of about 10 to 15 minutes from when you've put the items in your basket to when they will be confirmed – so it's important to only put items in your basket that you want to buy to avoid making any costly mistakes. The flowers are sold in wraps of around 20 to 50 minimum stems per variety. Most online wholesalers can source just about anything given a few days' notice.

WHOLESALE MARKETS

Usually, anyone can attend these markets and you'll find a variety of different wholesalers at them – just research where your local one is and set your alarm super-early if you want the best flowers because most of them will be gone by 9am! Here you can buy smaller minimum quantities and the flowers are sourced from all over the world, as well as from local growers. Being able to see and touch the flowers and discover new varieties is a huge advantage of going to a physical market. It's also a great way to form new relationships with suppliers and ask any questions you may have.

Local Flower Markets

Flower markets vary greatly, and I would encourage you to explore your local area and find out what's available to you. Some areas will have markets dedicated to cut flowers and plants such as Columbia Road Flower Market in London – a buzzy, bright and noisy market with bucketfuls of flowers as far as the eye can see. It's open every Sunday from 8am–2pm and you'll need to arrive early to secure the very best blooms. If you're looking to nab a bargain, arrive later as the traders start to reduce their prices to sell off their remaining stock. This is great if you're just looking for some flowers to play and experiment with, but if you want specific varieties and colours, then get there at opening time. In our local area, there are three small markets that each have one flower stall. Over the years, I have found some amazing flowers at really affordable prices, and I would arrange them over and over again to practise my technique, explore my style and photograph the designs.

Flower Farms

Sourcing directly from local growers is a magical experience – they often grow varieties you may never have seen or heard of before and the fragrance of some of the flowers is out of this world. In terms of reducing our carbon footprint and leaving minimal impact on our environment, this is a fantastic, sustainable way to source your flowers, as well as to support a local business.

Some flower farms are dedicated to producing just one type of flower, like dahlias for example, and others will grow a larger selection of flowers. The quantities they can provide are often smaller in comparison to wholesalers and be mindful that they are very reliant on the weather to help produce the best quality flowers when they're needed. It's a fabulous way to source your flowers but I would recommend that you are flexible about the varieties you want, and provide the growers with a choice of colours, or a mood board to work with and allow them to cut the best available blooms at the time you need them.

Growing Your Own Flowers

It doesn't get much more sustainable and cost effective than growing your own flowers. The joy that cutting a bucketful of blooms from your own garden and arranging them at home brings is incredibly rewarding. You don't need a huge space to grow your own flowers — existing garden borders, pots (ensuring they are big enough), or even a small window box are all great solutions. Here are some ideas:

- **Sweet peas** Grown from seeds and produce climbing vines with beautifully fragrant flowers in late spring. Pick these as often as possible to encourage more flowers.

- **Cosmos** Grown from seeds, with tall slender stems, wispy foliage and beautiful daisy-like flowers throughout summer. Pick and deadhead these as often as possible to encourage more flowers.

- **Dahlias** Grown from tubers planted in spring after the last frosts, these require a little more attention and time, but will reward you with incredibly beautiful and mesmerising flowers from late summer right through to the first frosts of autumn.

Foraging

Foraging is a great way to source flowers and foliage for your designs and I tend to choose stems that will add a natural and organic touch to my arrangements such as bare branches, blossom branches, dried seed pods, cow parsley, grasses and even some weeds.

The laws on foraging differ depending on where you are in the world, so research where you can forage and how to protect our ecosystem before cutting any flowers or foliage in the wild. To forage responsibly, always ask for the landowner's permission if you wish to pick from private land, never uproot a plant, and leave no trace that you've been on the land. Only cut from plants that are in abundance, leave plenty of flowers or foliage on the remaining plant and be aware of any protected species. Be sure to use clean, sharp scissors and cut as low into it as possible to help the plant recover and regrow (see page 25).

SELECTING YOUR FLOWERS

One of the things I love most about floristry is that it's ever-changing depending on the season due to flower availability. I can never decide which season is my favourite as each one comes with a bountiful supply of new and exciting stems to explore.

Once you are equipped with your tools, vases and vessels and your mind is buzzing with design ideas, it can feel a little overwhelming deciding which flowers to choose for your designs, as well as being sure that the flowers are available. Throughout each of the projects in this book, I have listed exactly what flowers and foliage I have used to create the designs, but I want to share my reasoning behind choosing those particular flowers to allow you to be able to choose alternatives and to create your own designs with confidence. To help guide you through this decision-making process, I have organised flowers into the four categories on the opposite page. You can find a comprehensive guide to my personal and most loved stems throughout the seasons in the Flower Directory on page 200.

When creating designs, I try to have a mixture of stems from all of these categories to ensure my arrangements are well balanced and packed with interest, texture and depth. There are of course circumstances where you may want to only use flowers from a couple, or just one of these categories. The Peony Mantel design on page 104 solely uses peony stems to create an abundantly rich and luxuriant arrangement. Many of the winter projects only incorporate foliage and a few filler stems for densely textured and natural designs. During the winter months I find myself drawn to foliage; the more varieties, shapes, and shades of green the better in my opinion to add maximum texture, fragrance and impact! I like to avoid rules and formulas when it comes to floristry, but I hope this helps you start to look at flowers and make an informed decision about which category you feel they fall into and then consider what their purpose and value are in your own designs.

Focal Flowers

The biggest showstopping blooms that command attention within your designs. I like to work these into my designs early on in the creating stage to make sure I am happy with their placement and that it feels natural and balanced.

—

Focal flower examples: peonies, hydrangeas, roses, dahlias

Supporting Flowers

These are the mid-way flowers in terms of size and also include tall and straight stems that add height and shape to your arrangements to support the large focal flowers.

—

Supporting flower examples: delphiniums, blossom branches, snapdragons, lisianthus, campanula, scabious

Filler Flowers

Here you'll find the most delicate stems that help pull a design together, fill in any gaps, conceal the mechanics and and enhance the final effect. While focal flowers help to draw the eye to the arrangement, the filler flowers can bring the designs to life by adding movement, depth and texture.

—

Filler flower examples: waxflower, astrantia, cow parsley, Ammi majus, orlaya

Foliage

Different varieties of foliage are available at different times throughout the year. Foliage is important for creating structure within an arrangement and to build a canvas for your flowers to stand out against. It can help define your design's shape, add colour, texture, and create harmony and balance between the flowers.

—

Foliage examples: trailing jasmine, ivy, grasses, olive, Eucalyptus populus

FLOWER CONDITIONING

The term 'conditioning' in the floristry world, simply means to care for your flowers. Understanding how to look after your flowers and so extend their vase life is crucial. For the vast majority of flowers, the following steps will apply. However, there are certain flowers that require slightly different methods of conditioning, and you'll find more on these on pages 24–25.

How to care for your flowers

1   It is vital that your buckets and vases are scrupulously clean so the flowers can effectively drink fresh, clean water. Dirty buckets encourage bacteria to build up, preventing the flowers from taking up water efficiently. I use warm water, washing-up liquid, a very small drop of household bleach and a good scrubbing brush to get them gleaming.

2   Fill your buckets/vases with fresh, tepid water. Ice-cold water is too harsh for your flowers to drink effectively, and having the water too warm will encourage the flowers to open more quickly. There may be some occasions where you need them to open faster, in which case this is fine — peonies are a great example of this.

3   Once the buckets are filled, add ¼ tsp of household bleach to the water and give it a swirl. The bleach helps to reduce bacteria growth in the water, thus helping the flowers' longevity.

4   It is important that you remove any unnecessary lower leaves from your stems. If any leaves sit below the water line, it will encourage bacterial growth and the freshness of the water will rapidly deteriorate. Also, by removing the unnecessary leaves, you are allowing the flower heads themselves to receive maximum hydration.

5   Cut 2.5–5cm (1–2in) from the ends of the stems at a 45-degree angle
     with sharp, clean floristry scissors. Cutting the stems at an angle simply
     increases the surface area from which the flowers can drink. Once cut,
     plunge the stems straight into the water – if you get distracted and forget,
     recut the ends of the stems.

6   Allow the flowers to have a good drink and rest for at least 12 hours
     somewhere cool and away from direct sunlight. I know all too well the
     temptation to get your hands on beautiful flowers straight away, but the
     benefits of allowing them to rest far outway the frustration at not being
     able to start arranging!

7   Re-cut the stems and refresh the water every 48 hours to allow your
     flowers to continue to drink fresh water optimally. Dispose of any wilting
     flowers as soon as you notice them as they will encourage bacteria build-
     up, affecting the other stems.

8   Clean and hide away your precious floristry scissors to stop anyone from
     using them to open the post!

Woody Stems

Woody flower stems and branches can be tricky to work with as the bark acts as a natural barrier preventing the stem from drinking the water it needs, so they are more prone to wilting. For flowering woody stems such as lilac, viburnum and hydrangea, remove as many of the leaves as you can allow for, to enable the stem to prioritise getting the water to the flower heads. Cut the stems at a 45-degree angle at least 2.5cm (1in) from the end, and then make a 5-cm (2-in) vertical slit up the stem from the bottom, further increasing the area from which the stems can absorb water. Use sharp, clean secateurs to create a neat cut that doesn't damage the stem or hinder its water uptake.

Plunge the stems immediately into fresh, tepid water and leave them in a cool, dark place. I find these stems always tend to drink the most, so keep an eye on the water level, particularly in warmer months.
—
Woody stems include: *viburnum, lilac, hydrangea, spiraea, forsythia, magnolia branches, blossom branches, beech, hornbeam*

Soft, Fleshy Stems

Stems in this category are usually found bursting into life in spring from bulbs that were planted in autumn. As these are often pulled straight from the ground, you may receive them with the bulbs and roots still attached (e.g. lily of the valley and tulips), or the white base of the stem (most commonly found on hyacinths). These stems cannot drink through the white base, so you must remove this by cutting just above where the white begins to turn green. Additionally, these stems prefer slightly cooler water than normal, and due to their 'fleshy' nature and heavy heads, the stems have a tendency to want to droop and bend – this is particularly noticeable in tulips. This can be magical to watch as they move and change shape in response to the light. However, if you require your stems to be a little straighter – e.g. for a hand-tied bouquet – then simply wrap them tightly in brown paper and plunge straight into water. The stems will become more rigid as they drink water and after 24 hours they will have straightened out.

Hellebores, while incredibly beautiful, can be particularly tricky to use as they often wilt prematurely depending on what stage of development they are at when picked. If the flower heads have all of their stamen still intact, they have not been fertilised, and are at their most delicate stage. To increase their longevity, using a sharp, clean knife, make a slit down the length of the stem, remove as much of the foliage as possible and plunge into fresh, tepid water. This extra cut increases the area from which the stem can drink, allowing it to hydrate as much as possible. Once the stamen have dropped and a seed pod has formed in the centre of the flower, you will notice a difference in the flower – the petals feel slightly waxy to touch and the stems are much more rigid and robust. These can then be conditioned as normal.

—

Soft, fleshy stems include: *tulips, fritillaria, hyacinths, hellebore, snowdrops, ranunculus, lily of the valley, narcissi, leucojum*

Sap-producing Stems

When these stems are cut, they secrete a thick, milky sap which can irritate the skin and affect other flowers nearby as the sap can block the base of the stems, thus limiting water intake. You may wish to wear protective gloves when handling such stems. For them to be safely mixed with other flowers in your designs, you must ensure the sap-producing stems are seared at the ends. Either pass the very ends of the stems through an open candle flame for a few seconds, or place them in freshly boiled water for a few seconds, and then place straight into cool water. Allow them to rest for at least 12 hours in water on their own before combining with other flowers.

—

Sap-producing stems include: *euphorbia, ficus, oxypetalum, poppies, narcissi*

Foraged Stems

Whether I'm cutting stems from our garden or from hedgerows out in the wild, I always try to carry a small bucket of water with me so I can cut the stems, strip away lower leaves, and pop them straight into water. This isn't always practical when you're out and about, so as soon as you can, condition your stems as necessary, recut the ends and plunge them straight into fresh, tepid water, allowing them to rest for at least 12 hours. It's best to cut stems early in the morning when they have had all night to become fully hydrated, and cut low down into the plant to give you the longest stem length as possible – not only does this help the plant regrow, but it also gives you a better stem length for arranging with. Generally, most flowers are best cut when they are just beginning to open and the petals are unfurling, revealing some colour. Note that if you cut flowers in full bloom, they will look beautiful initially, but will not last very long. On the other hand, if you cut flowers in tight buds, such as peonies or roses they may not fully open. (See page 19 for more on responsible foraging.)

STYLING ESSENTIALS

Choosing the Right Container

Container choice is fundamentally important to the overall effect of your flower arrangements. We could all be given the exact same bunch of flowers and the results could be totally different depending on the container we choose. Arrangements can easily look top heavy with a vase that's too small, or too tight and stiff with a vase neck that's too narrow. If you're just starting out with flower arranging, the vast choice of vases, bowls, jugs and pots may seem a little daunting, but a few simple tips can make this choice much easier and will transform the look and feel of your arrangements. To start with invest in a few classic vases and vessels that you can use time and time again to create varying arrangements throughout the seasons.

As a general rule of thumb, your arrangement should be approximately one and a half times the height of the vase and three times the width. There are obviously circumstances where you can break this rule, but I find this tip often gives people confidence as a basic starting point.

CLASSIC APOTHECARY VASE
Just about every day one of these vases is being used in our home. Its narrow neck and wide base are perfectly proportioned to support hand-tied bouquets and show off the spiralling stems. They're so versatile and are also ideal for angling stems in the vase so that they splay out to the sides forming a lovely shape. I like to use these on our kitchen island, dining table and coffee table, but thanks to their simplicity, they can be used just about anywhere you like.

OPAQUE SMALL LOW BOWL

Throughout this book you'll see me using various small bowls for different places in our home, from tablescapes to petite bedside-table arrangements. These low bowls require mechanics to support the flower stems. You can simply use a flower frog or chicken wire, or both. I love using small bowls to create light and airy arrangements with delicate small flowers to complement the size of the bowl.

BUD VASES

I have an ever-growing eclectic collection of bud vases that are slowly taking over my shed, from romantic and delicate shapes made from hand-blown glass, to left-over diffuser and perfume bottles. I have one rule when it comes to choosing a bud vase and that is to ensure the opening is narrower than the body of the vase to support the stems easily. The trend for using jam jars become popular some time ago and if you want to use these, pop little scrunched-up chicken wire inside to support the stems. This means you won't end up with flowers just around the edge of the jar and lots of empty space in the middle. Our kitchen sink is rarely without a simple bud vase with a couple of stems either from the garden or a left-over arrangement. For a more dramatic look, cluster small groups of bud vases together down the length of your table, or along your mantle, and fill with plenty of varied flowers of different heights. Slightly angle the stems in the vase to avoid them looking rigid and upright and make sure the size of the chosen flower is in proportion to the vase. The huge benefit of using bud vases is that they only take a few minutes to create – making them a popular choice. Some of my favourite stems for bud vases are freshly picked, fragrant sweet peas, soft and delicate panicum grass, a single garden rose, and a sprig of greenery such as olive, rosemary or eucalyptus.

OPAQUE VASE

I love using vases with texture and natural elements made from ceramic, cement, stone and terracotta to add warmth and interest. Often, these vases aren't watertight and so you may disregard them as an option for your fresh flowers. However, by simply putting a watertight container inside the vase, such as a cut-down milk carton or a drinking glass, you suddenly have a water source for your flowers. The beauty of using an opaque vase is that you don't need to worry about the stems' appearance as they won't be on show. If some of the stems don't reach the bottom of the vase, it doesn't matter as long as the stems comfortably reach the water. I choose these vases for large and dramatic arrangements for our sideboard, kitchen island or dining table to make a statement and draw the focus to the furniture.

LOW PLASTIC TRAYS

I came across these handy vessels a few years ago and thought they'd be ideal for an upcoming summer wedding where I was due to create a 20-seat-long fresh garland in a marquee and I was panicking about the heat and how well the flowers would last, and what mechanics I should use. Since then I have used the same trays over and over so many times and they work really well on our mantel and dining table to create beautiful long and low designs throughout the year. I simply fold a few layers of chicken wire into the trays, secure down with pot tape, fill with water and they're ready to use. These are ideal if you want to create low and long designs with movement and lightness. You'll see me using them multiple times throughout this book.

FOOTED PEDESTAL BOWLS/URNS

A simple foot can add elegance to a bowl, and footed vessels lend themselves perfectly to centrepiece designs. The best size to use is around 15cm (6in) tall with an opening no bigger than 15–17cm (6–6½in) for a console table, sideboard or dining table. I prefer an off-white ceramic bowl which suits all flowers and seasons. Footed vessels will require additional support such as a flower frog or chicken wire. You can make front-facing designs with these, such as the Asymmetric Urn Design (see page 152), or all-round designs, like the Asymmetric Spring Bowl (see page 52).

FINDING INSPIRATION AND DEVELOPING YOUR STYLE

Most of my inspiration comes from nature, whether it's a garden border, hedgerows, woodlands or somewhere I've travelled to or seen photographs of. A trip to our local garden centre can be inspiring too, as it gives me the opportunity to see seasonal plants and displays – I find it hard to go home empty handed, and I always leave feeling refreshed. It's easy to become complacent about the ordinary everyday things we see, but if you really stop to admire and acknowledge the shapes, textures, patterns and colours of the natural world, I believe you will find something to inspire you. Today, imagery and video content are right at our fingertips whenever we want – 3.2 billion images and 720,000 hours of video content are shared on social media every 24 hours! That so much information is easily available is wonderful in one respect, but it can also feel overwhelming at times, with almost too much to choose from when it comes to making your own decisions about style.

A wedding client once asked me how I would define my floristry style, and I immediately panicked. I'm unsure what words came out of my mouth in response, but it really made me start to question what my personal floristry style was. Up until that point, I was just grateful that clients wanted me to do their wedding flowers, or make them a wreath, so I gladly accepted, regardless of what style and colour palettes they chose. Of course there were some commissions that I really loved doing, but there were others where I just enjoyed the opportunity to work with flowers I wouldn't choose myself. It wasn't until I started experimenting more with the flowers I truly loved that my own personal style developed. Occasionally, this meant splashing out at my local florist, flower farm or wholesaler to get my hands on the most beautiful blooms, but it was worth every penny. From then on, I felt my style truly flourished, and I started to attract the type of work I really wanted, by sharing photos of my own designs on social media. My style is continually evolving, and what felt good five years ago has changed. Personally, I would become a little bored if I created the same designs and styles repeatedly; as I discover new techniques and flower varieties, I fall in love with floristry all over again.

Here, I wanted to share some of the things I've learnt over the years that may help you to find inspiration and to develop your own personal style. Flowers are there to be enjoyed and to help us express our creativity in whatever way that makes us happy.

Gathering Inspiration

• If you walk, drive or run around the same spots most days, ask yourself whether you really observe what nature is doing around you? If the answer is no, try doing that daily walk somewhere a little different and take the time to look and notice the shapes, colours and patterns within nature. Sometimes a little change to our routine is all we need to find new inspiration.

• Study your surrounding interiors and architecture. The best place to start with this is in your own home. Study the way the sunlight moves throughout your home during the day and consider how this affects the mood of the space. Is it a large or small space, and how can flowers complement the structures and interior that you already have? I can't look at a fireplace mantel without imagining all the ways to dress it with a huge foliage garland for the festive period, and a large round console table in a huge entrance hall with high ceilings always feels as though it is crying out for a tall, opulent vase arrangement. One of my favourite spots in our home to feature fresh flowers is on the kitchen island as it's a lovely light and bright spot and I spend a lot of time in this room. The kitchen is a bit of a blank canvas with neutral colours, no wall units on the back wall and two large clear glass pendant lights above the island. Adding flowers and greenery effortlessly adds life and interest to the space and breaks up the symmetry and straight lines in the kitchen, thus softening the overall feel to the room. Small rooms and little nooks lend themselves beautifully to considered and petite designs. We have a small side table in our reading nook by the fireplace and it's the perfect size for one of my small porcelain bowls holding an asymmetric floral design, such as the Garden Bowl on page 86.

• Use social media for inspiration. It could be a photograph of somewhere abroad where the colour combinations inspire a floral design, or a short video of grasses swaying in a woodland. Take screenshots or screen recordings of your favourite images and save them into albums on your camera role. I have four permanent albums in my camera role for spring, summer, autumn and winter where I have all my favourites saved in one easily accessible place. Pinterest is also a fantastic tool for creating inspiration boards, with a huge array of images and videos to discover.

- Take your own photos and videos when you're out and about. I probably take too many photos and can easily snap a hundred photos of cow parsley in the hedgerows when it's at its peak. Try to really look at the tiny details and the way things change throughout the seasons. Save your favourites to your albums to refer back to.

- Look through a child's eye – our two young daughters have taught me to be more in the present in the moment and to enjoy the little things in life. I think there is a lot to be said for how babies and toddlers view things as if for the very first time with such wonder and excitement! I have fond memories of taking our daughters for walks through the local park in their prams, and watching them gaze up at the huge trees above them and squealing with excitement. As we get older, naturally we become a little less curious and more complacent about our surroundings. But I would encourage you to acknowledge this and try to see things as if for the very first time, with renewed and fresh eyes.

- While the digital world of social media can provide constant inspiration, books and magazines are also a fantastic source of imagery that may be more specific to what you like. If you're crafty, you could try creating a scrapbook of your favourite images.

Developing Your Style

- Try not to force yourself into finding your own style and rather, focus your time and energy on creating designs that you are really proud of and love. The rest will naturally follow.

- Study other floral designers' work and see what types of designs you find yourself gravitating towards. Do you like wild and whimsical styles, neat and formal, or big, bold and bright? There is no right or wrong here, and there are no set 'styles' that you have to label yours as. It's fun to keep exploring other designs and styles as you may discover something you love that you'd not previously considered.

- Workshops are great places to connect with like-minded people, as well as to experiment with seasonal stems and create new designs. When choosing a workshop, I recommend researching the florist's style by having a look at their website and social media pages and ensuring you like their designs and flowers they use.

- Consider your fashion and interior home decor choices. Do you love to wear bright and patterned clothing to reflect a happy mood, or do you prefer to keep your style minimalist and monochrome? Do you have a favourite room in your home? If so, try and pinpoint exactly what it is about this space you love the most to help you understand your unique style.

◆ Be true to yourself, and have confidence in what you love, allowing yourself to explore your own personal style.

◆ Allow your style to evolve in whatever way feels right to you.

It's important to mention here that if your flower journey grows into something you'd like to take a little more seriously and start a business from, then developing your own authentic style is immensely important so that potential clients know what to expect and can define your brand image. If flowers are more of a hobby that you enjoy in your spare time, then developing your own unique style may not be as much of a priority to you, but still something that is fun to explore. I started The Suffolk Nest with one clear aim; to make flower arranging accessible to everyone, no matter what your experience. It has brought me so much joy over the past few years to see my designs being replicated throughout your homes whether it be from one of my seasonal wreath kits, or something we've created together on a live floristry tutorial on a Friday night. I love creating designs that you can replicate if you wish to, but also adapt to your own unique style.

HOW FLOWERS MAKE A HOME

I mentioned my passion and enthusiasm for home interiors earlier, and I have learnt over the years that while it feels important at the time (and believe me, it really did!), it didn't really matter what shade of white I eventually choose for our kitchen walls. What really matters are the little things that make a house feel like a home, and for me, flowers play a huge role in this. From my knowledge, this feeling of 'home' differs for everyone based on our experiences and tastes, and therefore, I hope that whatever flowers you choose to have in your home, they ignite joy. One of the things I love most about flowers is their fleeting nature, which is a beautiful and constant reminder that life is short, and to enjoy it whilst it lasts. So please, choose the flowers that bring you the most joy and happiness.

Dressing the dining table with fancy napkins and elaborate flower arrangements has given me great pleasure ever since my husband Chris and I had our very first guests over. I remember the first time we hosted Christmas Eve and I was so excited to extend our dining table, light all the candles and gather everyone around a beautiful setting. I made hyacinth planters topped with moss and dotted bud vases of white roses and garden foliage down the table laid on a crisp white linen tablecloth. Today, the scent of hyacinths always takes me right back to that magical Christmas Eve dinner. The flowers become a talking point and more recently our little girls will ask for the names of the flowers and make sweet remarks about them over dinner.

I have a particularly fond memory of bringing our youngest daughter home from hospital and being welcomed by our eldest daughter handing me a beautiful fresh pink peony. That week, almost every vase in the house (and there are a lot!) was filled with fluffy pink peonies — I've always loved them, but even more so now because of this memory I will cherish.

I like to regularly change and refresh our home interiors to reflect the seasons and our mood. After winter, as we move into spring and summer, I find myself

craving fresh, light and airy décor to enjoy the long sunny days. I pack away the heavy blankets, swapping them for light-weight knits, and switch soft furnishings to cottons and linens with subtle patterns. My floral designs in our home also reflect this change in mood, favouring a neutral colour palette, bringing some of the outdoors in by creating planters in early spring and designing light, airy designs in summer. During sutumn, as we retreat inside our homes, I seek to add warmth and cosiness into our interiors by using earthy stone vases, layering soft blankets and adding textured cushions to sofas and beds. My floral designs become more densely compact, and I like to add interest and depth using foraged seed heads and branches.

For me, the act of making a fresh wreath for our home signifies the start of a new season, and as the girls grow up, I hope to make it a tradition that we do together. You will find four completely different wreath designs within this book for each of the seasons, and I hope they inspire you to have a go at creating one for yourself, to suit your home.

SPRING

Spring feels like a huge sigh of relief after the dark, cold winter months. The clocks change, making the days longer and lighter, and new life begins to unfurl as fresh green shoots start to appear in the garden from the highly anticipated tulip bulbs planted in autumn. It signals a time for renewal, and I often find myself swapping out darker home furnishings for lighter and brighter choices to refresh and uplift our home, as well as flinging open the windows and doors seeking a connection with nature. The enjoyment of more relaxed entertaining takes place with the long Easter weekend to gather with loved ones and feast on seasonal food, while making new traditions and memories to last a lifetime.

Spring is a glorious season for flowers with a vast array of colours and masses of texture to work into your designs. Some of my favourite spring flowers include flowering branches from viburnum, lilac and various blossoms, packed with texture, colour and beautiful scent, and the delicacy of a single fritillaria or ranunculus. It's during this season that I love to create indoor planters using white bulbs, moss and branches to bring some of the outdoors, indoors.

After the long winter months, I love to bring new life and beautiful natural fragrance into our home with this spring planter. These are really simple yet so effective and will give you weeks of pleasure.

INDOOR SPRING PLANTER

WHAT YOU'LL NEED

- watertight container, any size or shape you like
- gravel
- multipurpose compost

Selection of bulbs and plants, such as:
- 2 white hyacinth
- 1 daffodil 'Bridal Crown'
- 1 fritillaria
- 1 trailing ivy
- 2 white muscari
- 6 white and purple pansies
- living carpet moss
- a few tall contorted willow branches
- a few pussy willow branches
- a handful of blown quail's eggs

METHOD

1 Add a thin layer of gravel to the bottom of the watertight container to aid drainage.
2 Remove the plants from their containers, ensuring they've had a good drink in the few days prior, and arrange them in the container until you're happy with their placement. I grouped the taller plants together in the middle and used the lower ones on the outside so they could be seen more easily. Position the trailing ivy on the edge to allow it to flow over the sides.
3 Fill in the gaps by packing the compost in and around the plants.
4 Cover the compost with the carpet moss. Simply tear it into shape and push it into any gaps.

→

5   Insert the willow and pussy willow branches into the moss and compost to create height and shape. I love using contorted willow for this as its curly nature creates a beautiful shape above the plants.

6   Finish by decorating with a few quail's eggs on top of the moss.

7   Position in a bright spot that's not too warm. Water every few days – I recommend using a long-spouted watering can for ease – but be careful not to overwater.

TOP TIPS

Once the bulbs have gone over, simply snip away the flower stems, leaving the leaves on, and they can then be removed and replanted outside to enjoy the next year. If some bulbs go over before the others you can replace them to enjoy your planter for longer.

I absolutely love celebrating Easter with my family and, just like Christmas, I like to go all out on the table decor. Here I've chosen some of my all-time favourite spring flowers including delicate lilac, anemones, sweet peas and hellebores to create a light and airy design using simple, sustainable techniques.

SPRING TABLESCAPE

WHAT YOU'LL NEED

- 3 small opaque bowls, approximately H8.2cm (3¼in) x D14.2cm (5½in)
- chicken wire
- pot tape
- floristry scissors
- 10 clematis 'Amazing Miami'
- 6 white lilac
- 6 purple lilac
- 8 double white hellebores 'Ellen White'
- 10 white allium 'Neapolitanum'
- 10 blossom stems
- 10 anemones 'Galil'
- ½ bunch white genista
- 15 white sweet peas

METHOD

1   Carefully scrunch up the chicken wire to create 3–4 layers that will fit inside the bowls. Place the wire into the bowls and secure with clear pot tape in a cross overlapping the sides by approximately 1–1.5cm (½–⅝in).

2   Fill the bowls three-quarters full with fresh, tepid water.

3   Position the bowls evenly along the length of your table. I like to create the arrangements in situ as it's easier to get a sense of scale and proportion; just be careful not to make too much mess if you have a tablecloth on the table.

4   Starting with the largest flowers (likely to be the lilacs), cut the stems to the desired height, position them in the bowls and arrange the chicken wire to support them. I used 2 or 3 stems in each bowl and had some lower down and some a little more raised.

5   Continue adding the flowers to the bowls, using the largest first and the smallest and most delicate to finish (the sweet peas were the final variety I added).

6   Remember to keep stepping back to make sure you're happy with the shape and flow of the tablescape. I wanted there to be plenty of space between the flowers to create a very natural, delicate and pretty design.

TOP TIPS

- Ideally the bowls should be roughly the same size, but it's nice if they don't match and all have their own uniqueness.
- It's easy to forget to top the water up when using opaque containers. Use a long-spouted watering can to water with ease.
- If you want to move your design after you've had a lovely dining experience, these little bowls look beautiful on bedside tables or side tables.

Spring is my favourite time to create beautiful asymmetric bowl designs using all the gorgeous blooms the season has to offer. The colours of this arrangement were inspired by the *Fritillaria persica* with its deep aubergine tones and small pop of yellow in the centre of the big bell-shaped petals.

ASYMMETRIC SPRING BOWL

WHAT YOU'LL NEED

- chicken wire
- footed bowl
- pot tape
- floristry scissors
- 8 *Fritillaria persica*
- 4 forsythia branches
- 10 frilly white tulips 'Cambridge'
- 10 purple parrot tulips 'Dark Parrot'
- 20 hellebores 'Camana Dark Pink'
- 20 fritillaria
- 10 daffodil 'Snow Paradise'
- 10 daffodil 'Pink Perfection'
- ½ bunch yellow genista
- 5 contorted willow branches

METHOD

1   Carefully cut the chicken wire to suit the size of the bowl and scrunch it up to create 5–6 layers. Place the wire into the bowls and secure with clear pot tape in a cross overlapping the sides by approximately 1–1.5cm (½–⅝in).

2   Fill the bowl three-quarters full with fresh, tepid water

3   Create the initial shape using 4 of the *Fritillaria persica*. Their stems usually have lovely bends that help create a unique and beautiful shape. Insert the stems into the bowl allowing the chicken wire to support them.

4   Cut the forsythia branches to size and insert into the chicken wire to continue to build the initial shape, aiming for more height on one side.

→

5 Add in the tulip, hellebore, fritillaria and daffodil stems following the shape you've created. Avoid placing the flowers in a line – play around with their height and positioning. It's nice to have some flowers deeper into the arrangement to draw the eye in, and some taller that almost dance above the display. Remember to keep standing back from your design and turning it around to see how it's building from all angles.

6 Add in the yellow genista (I stripped down the side shoots on their stems to make them much lighter to avoid any solid colour blocks).

7 Finally, add the contorted willow branches to complement the overall shape of the design.

TOP TIPS

Take your time and consider each flower's placement carefully. Walk away from the design for a few minutes and come back to it with fresh eyes to see the gaps and opportunities.

This is the perfect way to use up any stems left over from a larger project. Fresh flowers in the bedroom may seem a little decadent, but waking-up to such beauty is a real treat. I've used a floral frog here – I highly recommend having at least one of these in your tool kit as they're inexpensive and hugely versatile.

MINI SPRING BOWL

WHAT YOU'LL NEED

- flower frog, approximately 6cm (2½in) in diameter
- small bowl
- chicken wire
- pot tape
- 3 blossom branches
- 2 hellebores 'Winterbells'
- 2 white ranunculus 'Courchevel'
- 1 viburnum stem
- 3 white sweet peas
- 2 white alliums 'Neapolitanum'
- 1 daffodil 'Paperwhite'
- 3 white fritillarias

METHOD

1 Place the flower frog at the bottom of the bowl. Carefully scrunch up the chicken wire to create a couple of layers that will fit inside the bowl. Place the wire into the bowls and secure with clear pot tape in a cross overlapping the sides by approximately 1–1.5cm (½–⅝in). Fill the bowl three-quarters full with fresh, tepid water.

2 Begin with the blossom branches and hellebores to create the shape. Poke these directly into the pins on the flower frog to firmly secure them into a position you're happy with.

3 Once you're satisfied with the shape, add the ranunculus, positioning one low onto the rim of the bowl and the other slightly higher, facing the other way. As this is a front-facing design, you don't need to worry about the back.

→

4   Next add the viburnum stem — these can have up to 8 large snowballs of flower heads, so you may need to cut the stem down into smaller lengths to ensure they are in proportion to the bowl.

5   Continue to add in the flowers starting with the largest and working your way down to the smallest, following the shape you've created.

6   If you have any left over, add a few side shoots from the ranunculus stems to add some height and drama to the design.

TOP TIPS

As this design is very petite to suit its placement on a small bedside table, it's important to use flowers that are in proportion. Less is more here and you don't want too many stems, which will overcrowd the design. Ensure the flowers you select are delicate and compact.

There are some flowers that perfectly lend themselves to being arranged en masse, and lilac is one of them. Its cone-shaped panicles covered in tiny tubular flowers are dense yet delicate, and packed full of beautiful fragrance, texture and colour.

KITCHEN JUG

WHAT YOU'LL NEED

- jug measuring approximately H31cm (12½in) x W17.5cm (7in)
- 8 viburnum stems
- 35 lilac stems, a mixture of white and pale purple

METHOD

1 Fill the jug with fresh, tepid water
2 Start with the viburnum stems. Remove any leaves and flowers that will sit below the lip of the jug. Cut the stems at a sharp angle and place all the way around the jug at slightly varying heights to avoid them looking too symmetrical. I used 6 stems at this point, keeping back 2 for the middle of the jug.
3 Use the light purple lilac first. Cut the stems at a sharp angle and start placing in the jug to mingle with the viburnum. Place some higher and some lower and deeper into the viburnum to create a textured and frothy design.
4 As this is a 360-degree arrangement, keep turning the jug to make sure you're happy with it from all angles.
5 Then add in the white lilac, ensuring that the colours aren't blocked, but evenly distributed. Add the remaining viburnum stems to the middle of the jug so that they are evenly distributed throughout the arrangement.
6 Once all of the flowers are placed, take a step back and make any necessary adjustments.

TOP TIPS

Viburnum stems can easily become floppy
if it is too warm, or they need more water.
If they do look a bit floppy, they usually
perk up quickly after a good snip (about
2.5cm/1in) off the ends and a water refresh.
For this reason they're best positioned out
of direct sunlight in a cool spot.

This is probably the most technical wreath in the book, but I would urge everyone to give it a go, no matter your level of experience. It's created on a mossed base and as much of it is 'living' it will continue to grow and bloom – it's a joy to watch the changes over time.

SPRING WREATH

WHAT YOU'LL NEED

- 30-cm (12-in) wreath base (this could be a wire base, rattan base, or one you've created yourself from pliable branches such as clematis vine or willow)
- mossing wire or twine
- sphagnum moss
- water vials
- 3 muscari bulbs
- 2 hyacinth bulbs
- 1 small white primrose plant
- 1 small white pansy plant
- 10 fritillaria
- 3 double white tulips
- 4 daffodil 'Paperwhite'
- 6 hellebores
- 1 bunch olive stems
- 1 bunch pittosporum
- ½ bunch rosemary
- 6 pussy willow stems
- 2 contorted willow branches
- 3 blossom stems
- a handful of blown quail's eggs
- glue gun (optional)

METHOD

1 Attach the wire or twine to the wreath base. If you're using a wire frame (as I have), it's a good idea to create a zig zag pattern with the wire or twine to make a base for the sphagnum moss to sit on.

2 Add a chunky layer of sphagnum moss to the wreath base and secure it by taking the wire over and under the frame the whole way around. Keep the wire attached to the wreath.

3 Separate the bulbs, shake off any compost and run the roots under a tepid tap to remove any remaining compost. Lay the bulbs onto the wreath in a formation you're happy with. Keep in mind that the bulbs may grow taller, so consider the height they will grow to when positioning them.

4 Meander the wire around the tapered point of the bulbs – you may need to lift some of the foliage to avoid damage. Take your time and ensure they are secure. Once they're all attached, leave the wire attached to the wreath.

5 Wrap the bases of the primrose and pansy plants in a little damp sphagnum moss and attach to the wreath base using the wire.

→

6   Fill the water vials two-thirds full with fresh, tepid water and place the lids back on. Choose the flowers you'd like to add to your wreath and gently push the stems into the vials. You can insert more than one stem into each vial at varying heights – if you need to make the hole in the lid a little bigger, simply cut a small slit.

7   Position the flowers on top of the wreath base, filling in the gaps between the bulbs and plants. Cover the vials with a little sphagnum moss and then use the wire to secure.

8   Once all of the flowers, bulbs and plants are secure, fill any gaps with the foliage. Cut the foliage down to lengths of around 15–20cm (6–8in) and insert the stems directly into the wreath base at a slight angle.

9   Stand back and check you are happy with the shape and fullness, making any adjustments as necessary. Cut the pussy willow and contorted willow branches down to the desired size and insert into the sphagnum moss at an angle in the same direction as the foliage.

10 To attach the quail's eggs you can either use a glue gun, or wire them like I have here. Simply poke the wire carefully through the egg, bring the lengths of wire down, twist them around each other as close to the egg as possible and then insert the lengths of wire into the wreath base.

11 Finally, attach a length of twine to the top of the wreath for hanging.

12 Generously spritz the back of the wreath directly onto the sphagnum moss every 2–3 days to keep the foliage hydrated and the bulbs growing. The water vials can be topped up using a long-spouted watering can. Once the flowers have gone over, they can easily be removed and replaced with fresh flowers.

TOP TIPS

- This is a messy wreath to make, so give yourself plenty of room and have the compost bin close by so you can tidy as you're working.
- I prefer to work in a clockwise direction around the wreath and insert the stems at an angle to create a circular shape accordingly.

When the cherry blossom comes into bloom I love to use a few branches to form the structure of a bouquet. The pale pink blossom inspired the colour palette here using a spectrum of dreamy pink tones from ranunculus, double tulips and hyacinths, through to deep burgundy from the scabious.

SPRING HAND-TIED BOUQUET

WHAT YOU'LL NEED

* 3–5 blossom branches
* 6 pink butterfly ranunculus
* 10 pale pink ranunculus 'Hanoi'
* 5 pink double tulips 'Jonquieres'
* 8 deep burgundy scabious 'Bon Bon Scoop Merlot'
* 5 white alliums
* 5 pink hyacinths
* 7 pink double hellebores 'Ellen Pink'
* twine
* floristry scissors
* ribbon

METHOD

1   Begin by preparing your stems, ready to work with. Remove any foliage that would sit below the tie point of the bouquet and lay them on a flat surface in front of you. I like to group them by variety so I can easily pick the stems and see what I have left while creating the bouquet.

2   Prep your twine to tie off the bouquet – make a loop at one end of the twine and leave a length of around 7.5cm (3in) from the loop, and the other length about 20–25cm (8–10in) long (by prepping this beforehand, you don't need to worry about cutting and tying the string when you only have one hand spare).

3   Pick up the blossom branches and study their shape and movement. It might take a few attempts before you find a shape and composition that works, but it's best to get it right at this stage as these branches will form the overall shape of your bouquet. Aim for them to form a triangle shape where the highest point is in the middle, and the lowest is around the sides. Hold the stems securely with your non-dominant hand.

→

4   Next, start adding in your flowers. I used the
     tallest stems first, in this case the butterfly
     ranunculus, to follow the shape of the
     branches and start filling the bouquet out. At
     this stage, keep the bouquet still in your hand
     and poke the flowers into your hand as if it
     were a vase.

5   Add in the pale pink ranunculus and double
     tulips. As these are the largest flowers,
     it's important to get their positioning right
     throughout the bouquet. Ensure they feel
     balanced and well distributed with varying
     heights and depths – this will help add texture
     and interest.

6   At this point, the bouquet should start to feel
     more robust in your hand and you should
     now be able to turn the bouquet to work
     on all sides and angles more easily. As you
     continue adding in the flowers, simply pass
     the bouquet into your other hand and turn it
     slightly clockwise if you're right-handed, or
     anticlockwise if you're left-handed, and then
     hand it back to your non-dominant hand. This
     turning motion allows you to easily access all
     parts of the bouquet, as well as giving a neat
     finish to your stems.

7   As you work your way towards the end of
     the bouquet, start to bring the positioning
     of the stems lower to create a dome shape.
     I recommend using your shorter stems at
     this point, in this case, the hyacinths and
     hellebores worked well.

     →

8   Once you're happy with your design, take the length of twine you prepped at the beginning and hook the loop over your little finger that's holding the bouquet. Wrap the longer length around the bouquet and take it through the loop. Pull the length of twine back on itself and go around again to meet the other length of twine and tie a knot that's tight and secure.

9   Have a little measure up against your chosen vase and trim the ends of your stems over a bin using sharp, clean floristry scissors. It's always better to leave them too long and be able to cut more off, than to have taken too much off. Ideally you want the lowest flowers of the bouquet to touch the rim of the vase. The stems are too long if the bouquet tilts to one side of the vase.

10 Wrap your ribbon around the tie point to cover the twine and simply knot the it in place.

TOP TIPS

◆ As with any design, you may find as you go along that a particular flower you'd planned on using doesn't quite work (as for the bright pink tulips here, see page 73). Simply swap out the flowers and save them for another arrangement.

◆ This hand-tied technique is a little trickier than the tradition spiral and may feel awkward at first trying to get the flowers into position, but it's certainly worth your time and patience.

This design may look complex, but the foundations are very simple; it's just about using the branches you have to the best of their ability. Depending on the look you want to achieve, you could create this design on a smaller scale using the same technique and ingredients.

SPRING MANTLE

WHAT YOU'LL NEED

- secateurs
- 70–80 water vials with lids (see Top Tips on page 79)
- mossing wire
- 2–3 shallow bud vases
- 15–20 contorted willow branches
- 10 foraged blossom branches
- 10 daffodil 'Snow Heaven'
- 10 daffodil 'Pink Charm'
- 10 daffodil 'Paperwhite'
- 20 white double tulips
- 20 white ranunculus

METHOD

1   Start by conditioning the blossom branches (see Top Tips on page 79), if needed, the day before you plan to create your design.

2   Look closely at the contorted willow branches. Study their shape and consider where they best lend themselves to create your desired shape (I wanted my design to feel as though it was climbing up and along the mantle).

3   Once you have a rough idea, start placing and balancing the branches on top of your mantle. Take your time and position them carefully. You'll notice that the branches intertwine, which comes in very handy as it holds the design together. When you are happy with the position of the branches, move down to work on the side of the fire surround – I used two sturdy contorted willow branches balanced on the floor and against the fire surround.

4   Step back from your design and ensure you are happy with the shape. Ideally you want it to look natural with no obvious gaps or dense areas.

→

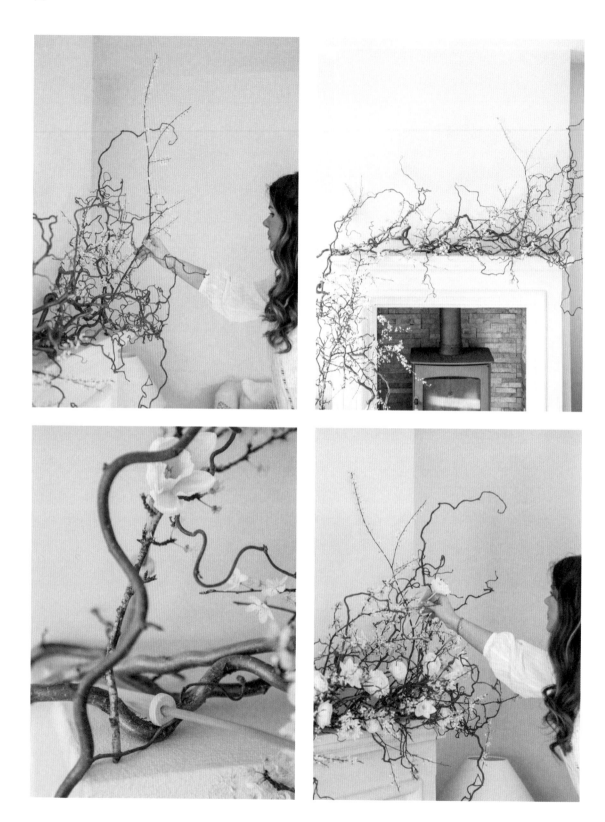

5   Next, place the blossom branches into water vials, if using (see Top Tips below). Simply remove the lid, fill the vial two-thirds full with fresh, tepid water, pop the lid back on and gently push the stem into the vial. Carefully intertwine the blossom branches onto the willow branches.

6   Once you're happy with the branch foundation, place every fresh flower stem into a water vial in the same way as the blossom branches. Once all the flowers have a water source, you can enjoy positioning them wherever you like. Consider the length of the stems, as it's nice to have some taller stems to add height and some much lower in the design.

7   Use the mossing wire to attach the vials to sturdy branches at the side of the design to give the appearance that the flowers are floating.

8   For the base of the design, fill the bud vases with layered mossing wire and add in as many of the fresh flowers as you like.

TOP TIPS

◆ If the blossom branches will fit into the water vials, it is beneficial to use them as the blossom will last longer. If not, you'll only need enough water vials for the flower stems.

◆ To condition the blossom branches, cut away the ends at a 45-degree angle using the secateurs and then create another cut (not cutting all the way through this time) about half way up the length of the branch. This will increase the cut surface area and allow the branches to take up more water. Plunge the branches straight into fresh, tepid water and leave overnight to hydrate before working with them.

SUMMER

When the sun shines and the trees are a lush green, it's time to embrace outdoor living – whether you're alfresco dining, picnicking on the beach or watching the sky become ablaze with a beautiful sunset. Social gatherings peak in the summer for many of us as our homes fill with children on their school break, family visiting from afar and friends stopping by. Fresh ingredients are at their finest during the summer months and I love nothing more than long relaxed barbecues in the garden with the doors flung wide open.

We are spoilt for choice with the array of flowers available at this time of year. My all-time favourite has always been, and always will be, the peony, with its showstopping ruffles and extraordinary colours; you'll find lots of uses for them in this chapter. I also love delicate and fragrant sweet peas, which are a complete joy to grow and can be snipped almost daily at their peak. At this time of year I find myself drifting away from dense foliage and choosing light, billowy grasses for small touches of green to add movement and interest to designs.

The placement, proportions and stem choices are very important with this design, so don't worry if you don't get it right first time – enjoy the process and take your time. The bowl I've used is small but perfect for this project and I've chosen flowers that are delicate and light to complement it.

GARDEN BOWL

WHAT YOU'LL NEED

- small bowl, approximately H8cm (3¼in) x W14.5cm (5¾in)
- chicken wire
- flower frog that fits comfortably at the bottom of the bowl
- floral fix
- pot tape
- floristry scissors
- 2 jasmine stems
- 2 orange blossom branches
- 4 ivory garden roses (cut from our garden)
- 3 pale yellow garden rose 'Royal Park' in bud
- 2 orlaya
- 3 asclepias
- 4 white scabious
- 5 chasmanthium grass stems
- a handful of daisies (picked from the garden)

METHOD

1 Take a small ball of floral fix and press it onto the back of the flower frog then gently push the flower frog down at the bottom in the centre of the bowl until it is secure.

2 Scrunch the chicken wire to neatly fit inside the bowl to create a few layers of extra support above the flower frog. Secure this in place with pot tape in a cross shape overlapping the the sides by approximately 1–1.5cm (½–⅝in) and fill the bowl three-quarters full with fresh, tepid water.

3 Begin forming your desired shape with the jasmine and orange blossom branches, removing most of the leaves from the orange blossom to give it longevity and keep it looking delicate. Press the branches into the flower frog to secure in place.

4 Next, add in the ivory garden roses and purposefully position these close to the rim of the bowl and further into the design. You want the roses to draw the eye in and allow the rest of the flowers to be light and airy.

5 Gradually add in the remaining flowers and grass to fill in the shape, carefully considering the height, proportion and balance of each stem. Often for this design, less is more.

6 Keep the water level topped up by using a long-spouted watering can.

TOP TIPS

After you've arranged just under half your flowers, stand back and take a front-on photo of your design on your phone and study what you've created so far. I often find that I notice gaps and changes needed via a photo more easily than in reality.

Our bedside table makes the perfect cool spot for this wild, light and airy vase arrangement. It's an absolute joy to wake up to on a summer's morning. Select a vase with an opening of no more than 14cm (5½in) so your stems are comfortably supported.

LIGHT AND AIRY VASE

WHAT YOU'LL NEED

- vase, approximately H25cm (9¾in) with an opening of 12cm (4½in)
- floristry scissors
- 3 elderflower
- 6 cow parsley
- 3 Clematis 'Amazing Vienna'
- 5 white delphiniums
- 4 *Ammi majus*
- 7 white veronica
- 4 panicum fountain grass

METHOD

1 Start by creating a shape that's in proportion to your chosen vase using the elderflower and cow parsley stems.

2 Add in the delphiniums for some height, ensuring the design isn't symmetrical to keep it feeling natural and wild. The beauty of no mechanics means you can easily remove a stem if you're not happy with it and recut or reposition if needed.

3 Continue to add in the remaining flowers following the shape of your design. Study the stems you have and decide where they will be best positioned. The *Ammi majus* stems have lovely large heads that fall forward, so pay careful attention to where these are placed so you can see the front-facing part of the flowers.

TOP TIPS

To keep the arrangement feeling wild and natural, resist the temptation to add too many flowers, even if you have more to hand. The space in between and around the flowers in this design is hugely important in creating a relaxed, hand-gathered feel.

It is always a challenge to create a fresh floral wreath with sustainable mechanics during the summer months, but I am absolutely thrilled with this abundant, vibrant design that made me fall in love with floristry all over again.

SUMMER WREATH

WHAT YOU'LL NEED

- water vials
- twine
- 30-cm (12-in) rattan wreath base
- floristry scissors
- 4 peony 'Dinner Plate'
- 4 peony 'Madame Claude Tain'
- 8 dahlia 'Wizard of Oz'
- 8 scabious 'Raspberry Scoop'
- 20 sweet pea 'Pink Wedding'
- 20 sweet pea 'White Wedding'
- 10 achilleas
- 10 limonium

METHOD

1   Prepare the water vials by filling them three-quarters full with fresh, tepid water and popping the lids back on. I then stand them upright in a large jug until needed.

2   Thread a length of twine through the top of the rattan wreath and secure with a double knot to hang. This will now be the top of your wreath and it's important to remember this while designing the wreath as the vials must remain upright to ensure the longevity of the flowers (see Top Tips on page 97).

3   Cut down the stems of the peonies at a 45-degree angle and insert each into a water vial, ensuring each stem is comfortably in the water. You want the flower head to sit close to the lids.

    →

4   Poke the water vial into the wreath base –
    it can take a little time at first to find the right-
    sized gaps in between the rattan, and you may
    feel that too much of the vial is on show, but
    once the design builds, they will be disguised.
    As you position the water vials, make sure
    you consider the side of the wreath and avoid
    creating any symmetry – particularly with the
    large flowers.
5   Next add the dahlias, scabious and sweet peas
    to the water vials, finishing with the achillea
    and limonium. For the slender stems (i.e. the
    sweet peas, achillea and limonium) use 2–3
    stems in each water vial to fill the gaps more
    easily and use fewer vials.
6   Remember to keep the vials topped up with
    water and replace any flowers that go over to
    make your wreath last as long as possible.

TOP TIPS

If you position a water vial upside down
at the bottom of your wreath, it may look
nice, but the flower won't last very long as
the water won't reach the end of the stem.
If you need to do this, choose hardy stems
and cut the stem shorter so it can more
easily drink water.

Fill a large jug with classic white and green flowers for all the impact without the effort. There are no special mechanics here, you just need a jug with a slightly tapered neck to support the stems. Once the more delicate stems have gone over, simply replace with different flowers to refresh the display.

CLASSIC JUG

WHAT YOU'LL NEED

- large jug with a slightly tapered neck, approximately H26cm (10½in) x W21cm (8¼in)
- floristry scissors
- 4 white foxgloves
- 2 climbing hydrangeas
- 5 white campanulas
- 3 spiraeas
- 5 white stock
- 5 lisianthus
- 5 orlaya
- 1 fully open white peony
- 2–3 white roses

METHOD

1. Start by forming the structure and shape of your design using the tallest foxgloves (ideally the tallest stem should be approximately one and a half times the height of the jug), ensuring their positioning feels natural.

2. Position the climbing hydrangeas in the jug to add mass lower down in the design and to fill out the shape.

3. Continue to add in a variety of stems, carefully following your chosen shape, saving the peony and roses to last.

4. Finally add in the peony just off to one side, resting on the rim of the jug, then arrange the roses. These are the focal flowers of the design and should be nestled into the jug once you're happy with the shape and structure.

5. Keep the jug topped up with plenty of water, especially if it's to be positioned in a warm kitchen, using a long-spouted watering can for ease.

TOP TIPS

Remember to step back from your design
regularly to see how everything is coming
together and assess whether there are
any gaps.

Peony season is fleeting, from late spring through to early summer for the best blooms, and I can never get enough of them! Here I have used a variety of pink peonies starting with the palest and most delicate soft shades, right through to a deep burgundy red tone to create warmth and depth in the design.

PEONY MANTLE

WHAT YOU'LL NEED

- Low watertight container or several containers measuring approximately L42cm (16½in) x W10cm (4in) x H5cm (2in) in total
- chicken wire
- pot tape
- glue dots
- 8 peony 'Highlight'
- 7 peony 'Old Faithful'
- 18 peony 'Nick Shaylor'
- 10 peony 'Mother's Choice'
- 10 peony 'Dinner Plate'
- 8 peony 'Bowl of Cream'
- 6 peony 'Sarah Bernhardt'

METHOD

1 Begin by prepping the mechanics. Cut the chicken wire to the same length as the low container and approximately five times the width.
2 Carefully fold the cut chicken wire about five times so it fits into the container and has created enough layers of support, but enough gaps to ensure you can insert your stems.
3 Secure the chicken wire into position using the pot tape, ensuring that the mechanics are robust and the chicken wire won't move.
4 Position glue dots along the bottom of the container and gently press the container down onto the mantle to firmly hold it in position.
5 Carefully fill the container three-quarters full with fresh, tepid water. I use a long-spouted watering can for this to avoid any spillages.
6 Cut the peony stems at a 45-degree angle.

→

7   Insert the largest, most open blooms into the chicken wire, ensuring that each stem is submerged in water.

8   Continue adding in the peony stems, allowing them the space they need, and keep them evenly distributed across the length of the design. Avoid creating any symmetry or lines with the flowers as this will look too structured and stiff – consider the height and angles of their positioning and stand back every now and then to see how the design is building and ensure the placement feels naturally random.

9   Once you're happy with the position of the largest blooms, add in the next largest flowers and work your way down to the smallest buds, following the shape of the design.

10 Top up the water in your container as frequently as needed.

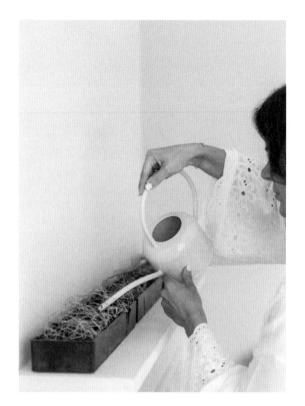

TOP TIPS

To encourage peonies to open, cut the stems at a 45-degree angle, remove as many of the lower leaves as you can, submerge into warm water, and place in a warm sunny place. You may notice some clear sap on the outer guard petals – this is completely normal, but too much of it may prevent the flower from opening. Gently massage the guard petals in a downwards motion to help get things moving.

This design, using intricate wire work and very short stem lengths, is one of the most technical in this book. Much like making a wreath or garland, once you've mastered the mechanics placing the blooms is pleasingly methodical, allowing you to lose yourself a little, and focus on the design.

MIDSUMMER CROWN

WHAT YOU'LL NEED

- base wire
- Stemtex tape
- floristry scissors
- ribbon
- 6 peonies
- 5 scabious
- 10 helichrysum
- 4 clematis
- 7 nigella
- 3 limonium
- 3 achillea

METHOD

1   Take the base wire and measure it around your head. I like to leave about a 15cm (6in) gap at the back to show off the ribbon and bow, but you can make it as long or short as you wish. Once you're happy with the length, make a small loop at either end by carefully wrapping the wire around something small and circular to keep the loop nice and neat. Twist the wire back onto itself.

2   Position the Stemtex tape at one end of the wire and pull on it slightly to activate the adhesive and tightly wrap all the way down the length of the wire. This will make it easier to attach the flowers.

3   Take a handful of mixed flowers and cut the stems at a 45-degree angle a few centimetres from the flower base and create a miniature flat fan-shaped bunch. Position the mini bunch to to cover one of the loops and attach it to the base wire using the Stemtex tape, ensuring the ends of the stems are covered to help lock in as much water as possible. Tear off the tape and flatten down the end.

→

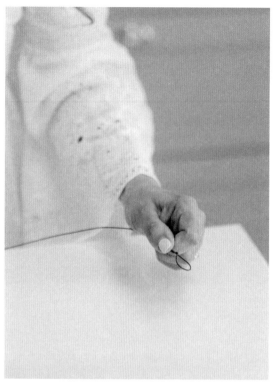

4   Gather your next mini bunch and attach this tightly against the first, in the same direction, ensuring none of the base wire is on show.

5   Continue this process down the entire length of the wire ensuring you're happy with your focal flower positioning. I try to use slightly different flowers from the previous bunch to add interest to the overall design.

6   Once you are near the end of the wire, you will have a gap before the loop as the bunches have all been attached in the same direction. To help cover the other loop, position one of the mini bunches in the opposite direction, covering the loops and attach this using the Stemtex. There will be a slight gap between this bunch and the rest of the crown, so carefully position another bunch here using a larger flower head and then fluff up the end to disguise any small gaps.

7   Finally, thread the ribbon through the loops ensuring the length is long enough to tie a secure, neat bow.

TOP TIPS

Make your crown as close as possible to when it will be worn to get the most longevity from the flowers.

This beautiful, big hand-tied bouquet is made using the classic spiral technique combining an array of textures, fresh and light colours, large focal blooms, delicate fillers and tall stems with movement. Once you've mastered the spiral technique, challenge yourself to see how big you can go!

SPIRAL HAND-TIED BOUQUET

WHAT YOU'LL NEED

- floristry scissors
- twine
- glass vase with tapered opening, approximately H25cm (10in) x W19cm (7½in) with a 14.5cm (5¾in) opening
- 4 foxgloves
- 4 lunaria
- 5 delphiniums
- 4 peonies
- 4 garden roses
- 4 agapanthus
- 6 alliums
- 4 clematis
- 6 astrantia
- 4 orlaya
- 4 scabious
- 5 nigella
- 6 chasmanthium grass
- 6 panicum fountain grass

METHOD

1   Begin by preparing the flower stems. Remove any foliage that would sit below the tie point of the bouquet and lay the stems out on a flat surface in front of you. I like to group them by variety so I can easily pick the stems and see what I have left while creating the bouquet.

2   Prep your twine to tie off the bouquet – make a loop at one end of the twine and leave a length of around 7.5cm (3in) from the loop, and the other length about 20–25cm (8–10in) long (by prepping this beforehand, you don't need to worry about cutting and tying the string when you only have one hand spare).

3   Choose your first ingredient and place it in your non-dominant hand between your thumb, index and middle fingers. I chose to use a tall foxglove stem – I find it easier to start with something longer, and I wanted the taller stems to be in the middle of the bouquet.

→

4   Choose your next ingredient (I used a stem of
    lunaria) and cross it over the first stem in your
    hand at a slight angle. This crossing over is the
    key to the stems creating the spiral.
5   Next, turn the 2 stems a full 180 degrees. Do
    this by turning them in your dominant hand and
    then passing them back to your non-dominant
    hand ready to add another stem. This will feel
    unnatural and a bit awkward at first, but as the
    bouquet builds it will become much easier.
6   Add in the next stem at the same angle to the
    first and repeat step 5. Take your time to do
    these stages properly. Focus on the flower
    heads, positioning and height. The stems will
    all vary in length at this point – do not worry,
    these will be trimmed and neatened at the end.
7   Hold the stems loosely – it doesn't matter at
    this stage if they fall down or around a little
    as you can easily pull them back up later. The
    action of adding in a stem at an angle, passing
    it to your dominant hand to turn it, and then
    passing it back to your non-dominant hand, is
    the secret to a successful spiral bouquet.
8   How far you turn the bouquet each time is
    likely to vary as you progress, and as you
    notice gaps, and spaces you want your flowers
    and foliage to sit. When you see gaps, look at
    your flowers and consider what will work best
    – does it need something tall and thin, large
    and round, or a small filler?
    →

9   As the bouquet builds, you will find it becomes much easier to add your stems and turn the bouquet and you will notice the stems are forming a beautiful spiral.

10 As you near the end of the bouquet, start to bring the flowers slightly lower down to form a dome shape. This is where I used the large focal flowers to ensure they could easily be seen from all angles.

11 Once you're happy with your design, take the length of twine you prepped at the beginning and hook the loop over your little finger of the hand that's holding the bouquet. Wrap the longer length around the bouquet and take it through the loop. Pull the length of twine back on itself and go around again to meet the other length of twine and tie a knot that's tight and secure.

12 Have a measure up against your chosen vase and trim the ends of your stems over a bin using sharp, clean floristry scissors. It's always best to leave them too long and be able to cut more off, than to have taken too much off. Ideally you want the lowest flowers to touch the rim of the vase. The stems are too long if the bouquet tilts to one side of the vase.

TOP TIPS

As the bouquet gets bigger, it will become heavier and harder for you to hold in one hand. If you struggle with this, you can tie your bouquet off loosely and then continue to add more stems, safe in the knowledge that everything is secure.

Here, I have chosen a fabulously vibrant colour palette of bright corals, soft peach, delicate pinks and deep burgundy to create a joyful summer feeling. The beauty of bud vases is that they can easily be moved, so when dinner is over, you can enjoy the flowers for longer throughout your home.

ALFRESCO TABLESCAPE

WHAT YOU'LL NEED

- floristry scissors
- bud vases, jam jars or small bottles to position down the length of your table (I used 22 vases for a 2.5m/8¼ft long table)
- 4 peony 'Coral Charm'
- 5 peony 'Sarah Bernhardt'
- 4 peony 'Old Faithful'
- 7 dahlia 'Wizard of Oz'
- 5 garden rose 'Vuvuzela'
- 5 garden rose 'Count Spirit Louise'
- 8 pink snapdragons
- 6 pink scabious 'Raspberry scoop'
- 10 sweet pea 'Rose Wedding'
- 10 sweet pea 'Pink Wedding'
- 10 strawflowers
- 20 chasmanthium grass

METHOD

1   Start by positioning the vases along the length of your table. I like to create small groups of varying heights together, so it feels naturally random. Fill the vases three-quarters full with fresh, tepid water.

2   Start by positioning your largest, focal flowers. I like to keep the larger flowers low and close to the rim of the vase to avoid the vase toppling over, and also feels more in proportion to the small vase. Think about the angles you position these at and avoid any symmetry.

3   Then add in the taller flowers (for me, these were the snapdragons and scabious). Check they aren't so tall that they'll obstruct the view of your guests. Once you've positioned a few stems, take a seat at the table and see how the height feels. If it obstructs your view, remove them and snip them down.

4   Then use your filler flowers to create lots of varying interest between the vases. They should all be different but have a sense of continuity to them and should complement each other.

124

TOP TIPS

If it's slightly breezy and you're worried the vases may topple over, pop some clear glue dots on the bottom of each one, and they won't budge.

AUTUMN

The turning of the leaves from lush greens to rusty reds and oranges; the drawing in of the days; the creeping in of colder weather. Autumn is a time when the natural world prepares itself for the winter months. It is a time of cosying-up, of crisp mornings and crunching through piles of leaves.

For me, autumn means retreating more into our homes after the summer season of holidays and outdoor living. Routines are picked up with the start of new school terms, candles are lit for the darker evenings, warm sweaters are dug out from drawers and hats start to make an appearance. Autumn is fast becoming one of my favourite seasons, bringing with it a whole new world of colour and texture to explore in my floral designs.

The grasses and seed pods have dried out after the hot summer, the shades of the leaves are fiery and warm and there's an abundance of thriving flowers to perfectly complement them. A few of my favourites are hydrangeas (the mellow, muted tones come into their own in autumn), chrysanthemums with their deep, rich colours and textures, and dahlias for something showstopping and special.

In the designs that follow you'll find ways of celebrating this beautiful season in your home using a variety of rich colours from aubergines, plums and burgundies to rusty oranges and muted, delicate pinks.

You can make this tablescape design to suit any length of table and can even display the sections throughout your home after the event. I've used a variety of mid- to late-autumn flowers, from large impactful dahlias to small, delicate, chocolate cosmos, to draw the eye in.

AUTUMN TABLESCAPE

WHAT YOU'LL NEED

- watertight opaque containers, ideally long and thin (plastic food containers with lids are great for this), measuring approximately L42cm (16½in), W10cm (4in), H5cm (2in)
- lengths of chicken wire, approximately 42cm (16½in) x 40cm (16in) for each container – the exact size will depend on the size of your containers
- pot tape
- floristry scissors

Selection of flower stems, such as:
- 40 clematis 'Amazing Kibo'
- 40 clematis 'Inspiration'
- 10 dahlias 'Dark Night'
- 40 ranunculus 'Nerone'
- 30 stock apricot
- 40 scabious 'Raspberry Scoop'
- 20 scabious 'Hanoi'
- 50 chocolate cosmos
- 20 astrantia 'Ballerina'

METHOD

1   Carefully concertina fold the chicken wire lengths to fit your chosen vessel to create 3–4 layers of wire.
2   Secure the chicken wire in place with pot tape – pot tape sticks very well to itself and becomes very secure.
3   Three-quarters fill your containers with fresh, tepid water. I find it much easier to do this in situ as the containers can be tricky to move once filled without spilling.
4   Start placing the flower stems into the container through the spaces in the chicken wire to build a base. I started with clematis stems as they were the densest, with more foliage compared to the others. Consider all angles and the height of the finished design. If you're creating something for a dining table, this design works beautifully when kept at a low height, so the flowers don't interrupt conversations over dinner.

→

5   Once you've built the base continue to add one variety at a time, starting with the largest blooms and finishing with the more delicate, smaller stems. After the clematis, I added the dahlias, then the ranunculus, stock and scabious. It works well to position some stems from the same varieties deeper into the design and some as a focal point to create a sense of depth and draw the eye in. Imagine you are sitting at the table and consider how the design would look.

6   As your design is building and you are nearing the end, start to ensure that all the chicken wire and pot tape is well hidden. I used the astrantia stems to help cover any last little bits of chicken wire – they're a beautifully delicate filler flower, and the colour suited this design perfectly.

7   I finished the design by adding in the stunning chocolate cosmos stems and left these a little taller so that some of the stems danced above the arrangement.

TOP TIPS

* Don't worry too much if some of the stems move around a little at the beginning – as you continue to add more flowers, the stems will hold their position more easily.

* Remember to top up the water. As the trays are shallow, the flowers will drink the water quickly and you may not necessarily notice as the trays are opaque. Use a long-spouted watering can to easily fill through the flowers.

Hand-tied designs build up much more quickly than traditional spiral bouquets, and once you've mastered this technique, you'll want to make these all the time. Here I used vibrant orange beech branches and foraged bracken to form my base and then added in other autumnal treasures to create texture, depth and interest.

HAND-TIED DESIGN

WHAT YOU'LL NEED

- floristry scissors
- twine
- velvet ribbon (optional)

Selection of flower stems and foliage, such as:

- 4 preserved beech branches
- 3 bracken stems
- 5 *Eucalyptus cinerea* branches
- 3 variegated ivy
- 2 chrysanthemum 'Vienna Copper'
- 3 chrysanthemum 'Avignon'
- 3 chrysanthemum 'Bigoudi Red'
- 3 chrysanthemum 'Doria Salmon'
- 2 rose 'Quicksand'
- 2 stems orange ilex berries
- 3 stems viburnum berries
- 4 echinacea seed heads
- 3 sanguisorba
- 5 panicum 'Warrior' grass
- 5 talinum 'Long John'

METHOD

1   Start by prepping all your ingredients by ensuring they've been well conditioned – remove all the lower foliage that would sit below the tie point and lay the stems down in front of you in groups by flower type. Spending a little time doing this means that when you're in the zone creating your bouquet, you always have the flowers easily to hand, while your other hand is busy holding the bouquet.

2   Prep your twine to tie off the bouquet – make a loop at one end of the twine and leave a length of around 7.5cm (3in) from the loop, and the other length about 20–25cm (8–10in) long (again, by prepping this beforehand, you don't need to worry about cutting and tying the twine when you only have one hand spare).

3   Choose the branches that will form the main shape of your bouquet – you're looking for interesting branches whose shapes complement each other. I used 4 beech and 3 bracken branches and held these in my non-dominant hand hand between my thumb, index and middle fingers.

4   Start adding to the design by poking other stems into your hand, almost using your hand as the vase to hold all the stems together. Remember to keep turning the bouquet around so you can see how it's building from all sides. I find this easier to do as the bouquet gets a

→

little bigger. I like to start with a foliage base, and then add in my largest blooms, working my way down to the smallest and most delicate stems – in this case, the order I used my ingredients in was as follows: eucalyptus, ivy, chrysanthemum 'Bigoudi Red', 'Vienna Copper' and 'Avignon', rose 'Quicksand', ilex berries, viburnum, echinacea seed heads, chrysanthemum 'Doria Salmon', panicum 'Warrior' grass and talinum 'Long John'.

5   Once you're happy with your design, take the length of twine you prepped at the beginning and hook the loop over the little finger of the hand that's holding the bouquet. Wrap the longer length around the bouquet and take it through the loop. Pull the length of twine back on itself and go around again to meet the other length of twine and tie a knot that's tight and secure.

6   Measure the bouquet against your chosen vase and trim the ends of your stems over a bin using sharp, clean floristry scissors, if needed. Remember that it's always better to leave the stems too long and be able to cut more off later, rather than to have taken too much off. Ideally you want the lowest flowers of the bouquet to touch the rim of the vase. The stems are too long if the bouquet tilts to one side of the vase.

7   I chose to add a deep red velvet ribbon, draped over the side of the vase, that complemented the colour of the 'Bigoudi Red' chrysanthemums. I love the contrast of this colour against the aged yellow pot.

TOP TIPS

Place a mirror in front of you before you begin and use it to check on how the shape and design is building from all angles.

Floating installations may look quite advanced and potentially intimidating, however the important thing here is to spend some time getting the mechanics right to put your mind at ease and then you can have fun with the flowers! This type of design is best created in situ as you get a much better sense of scale and transporting can be tricky.

DRIED FLOATING INSTALLATION

WHAT YOU'LL NEED

- approximately 1m (3¼ft) bamboo rod
- approximately 1m (3¼ft) x 4m (13ft) chicken wire
- clear cable ties
- fishing wire (the one I used was 0.6mm and holds up to 18kg/40lbs in weight)
- floristry scissors

Selection of dried flower stems and foliage, such as:
- 15 pampas grass stems
- 8 bunches dried honesty
- 8 bunches dried bleached ruscus
- 5 bunches dried flax
- 5 bunches dried broom
- 5 bunches dried white helichrysum
- 2 bunches dried muni grass
- 2 bunches dried bunny tails

METHOD

1   Start by building the mechanics for your installation. Choose the appropriate length of bamboo for the space you are working with. Note that your design will end up being larger than the mechanics.

2   Roll the chicken wire to create 3–4 layers (you may find it easier to slightly scrunch the chicken wire to achieve the layers).

3   Slide the bamboo rod through the chicken wire and attach it tightly to the chicken wire using clear cable ties at both ends and in the middle.

4   Attach 2 lengths of fishing wire to the bamboo and chicken wire frame at either end and hang it from the ceiling (I hung the frame from an old barn beam).

5   Snip away any lengths of fishing wire or cable ties that may be on show.

6   Now that the mechanics are in place, you can begin adding the flowers. I started by placing the pampas grass into the chicken wire to build the shape, carefully considering the design's appearance from all angles. I chose to have one side more exaggerated than the other to create an asymmetric shape to add interest to the finished design.

→

7   Once you're happy with the shape, start adding your next largest stems – in this case, the honesty and ruscus. Poke them into the chicken wire ensuring they are secure, varying the lengths to add interest and depth to the design. Don't worry if the stems move around a bit at this point; as you add more stems, they'll hold in place more easily.

8   Stand back from the design to see how it is building. Walk all the way around it, and even take a step away from it for a while and come back to it with fresh eyes a little later to see how you feel.

9   Next add the flax, broom and helichrysum. I played around with depth using these and had some stems much shorter and closer to the chicken wire frame. These stems are great choices for covering the chicken wire mechanics as well as complimenting the design by adding lots of texture.

10 Finally, add the muni grass and bunny tails. As these stems are so thin, you may find it easier to hold little bunches of 5–10 stems together, bluntly cut their ends and insert them into the chicken wire. I love how soft and light these dried flowers are and the way they add a whimsical magic to the design.

TOP TIPS

Depending on the size of your arrangement, a floating design is likely to use a lot of flowers. Take time to plan what flowers and foliage you'll be using to avoid under- or over-buying.

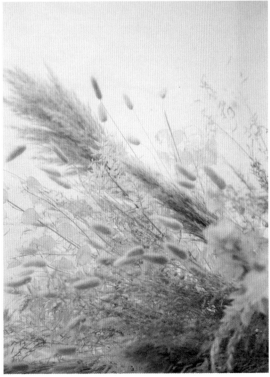

If you're lucky enough to have a hydrangea plant in your garden then I highly recommend having a go at drying the flowers yourself by simply snipping them in early autumn, removing all the leaves, placing them in a vase of water and leaving them to dry naturally for a couple of weeks.

HYDRANGEA VASE ARRANGEMENT

WHAT YOU'LL NEED

- ceramic vase, approximately H26cm (10½in) and D23.5cm (9¼in)
- 4 bunches *Eucalyptus parvifolia*
- 10–15 *Hydrangea paniculata*
- birch twigs
- floristry scissors

METHOD

1 Half fill your chosen vase with fresh, tepid water.
2 Arrange the *Eucalyptus parvifolia* in the vase as the base to build the shape of the design, using the largest branches first and filling spaces with the smaller ones. Remove any of the lower leaves to avoid them sitting below the water line as this helps reduce bacteria build-up.
3 Next, nestle the hydrangeas into the foliage base, using the largest stems first. It works well to have some that are lower and deeper into the foliage, and some that are taller and slightly prouder.
4 Finish the design with the birch twigs. You can use this to accentuate the shape as well as adding lots of texture and interest.

TOP TIPS

Consider where your finished design will be positioned. I love having mine either on our kitchen island or dining table to be admired from all angles. If this is the case for you, too, remember to keep turning the vase as you build the design to make sure it looks beautiful from all angles.

This rich, abundant wreath gives a lovely warm welcome to your home while perfectly depicting the season. There is so much choice of beautiful foliage and interesting textured ingredients – from berries and seed pods to leaves and twigs – I have no doubt that you'll find creating it truly therapeutic.

AUTUMN WREATH

WHAT YOU'LL NEED

- 30-cm (12-in) wreath base (this could be a wire base, rattan base, or one you've created yourself from pliable branches such as clematis vine or willow)
- mossing wire or twine
- sphagnum moss
- floristry scissors

Selection of foliage, such as:
- 1 bunch variegated ivy
- 1 bunch mimosa
- ½ bunch seeded eucalyptus
- ½ bunch *Eucalyptus parvifolia*
- 1 bunch pistache
- foraged bracken stems
- preserved beech leaves
- 7 stems viburnum berries
- 5 stems orange ilex berries
- 10 scabious seed heads
- 6 white waxflowers
- 10 talinum 'Long John'
- 10 red skimmias
- 5 echinacea seed heads
- velvet ribbon

METHOD

1   Attach the wire or twine to the wreath base. If you're using a wire frame (as I have), it's a good idea to create a zig zag pattern with the wire or twine to make a base for the moss to sit on.

2   Add a chunky layer of sphagnum moss to the wreath base and secure it by taking the wire over and under the frame the whole way around. Keep the wire attached to the wreath.

3   Cut all your foliage and decorative ingredients into workable lengths, roughly 15–25cm (6–10in) – you want a good mixture of shapes and sizes so don't worry too much about being precise.

4   Choose the direction you would like to work around your wreath. I find it most comfortable to work in a clockwise direction as I'm right-handed, but it really doesn't matter as long as you work in the same direction the whole way around.

5   Gather a handful of your ready-trimmed ingredients into a bunch in the shape of a fan.

6   Starting at what will be the top of your wreath, position the stems of the bunch in the centre of the moss-covered base and let the foliage fan out to cover the moss.

 →

7   Attach the bundle using your wire and wrap around the ends of the stems 2 or 3 times until it feels secure.

8   Continue to gather and attach bundles – I like to choose slightly different ingredients from the previous bundle to keep it interesting – positioning each bundle in the same direction and overlapping the previous bundle so that the wire and stems are covered.

9   When attaching the final bundle simply lift the foliage from the first bundle you created and tuck the stems of the last bundle underneath to conceal them.

10 Once all your bundles are attached, turn your wreath upside down, trim the wire at about 15–20cm (6–8in) and use it like a sewing needle looping back and forth across the wire frame until it feels secure.

11 Use any leftover ingredients to fill in any gaps or add additional texture.

TOP TIPS

◆ Keep the wire or twine taut as you work around the base.

◆ Keep the wire attached from start to finish.

◆ Step back from your wreath or have someone hold it up for you so you can see the shape building up and identify any gaps (for me, this turns what would otherwise have been an average-looking wreath into an impressive professional one).

◆ Poke additional ingredients into the mossed base for extra texture and interest.

◆ The number of stems and bundles used isn't particularly important so be guided by eye here.

When it comes to an asymmetric urn design, less is definitely more. It's easy to get carried away and continue adding more and more flowers, but if you really take your time with this and consider each flower and its placement carefully, you will create breathtaking designs that are delicate, romantic and truly captivating.

ASYMMETRIC URN DESIGN

WHAT YOU'LL NEED

- Watertight urn or footed bowl, approximately H19cm (7½in), W17cm (6½in), D14cm (5½in)
- chicken wire
- pot tape
- floristry scissors

Selection of flower stems, such as:
- 4 dried cow parsley
- 7 jasmine
- 3 hellebores
- 3 garden rose 'Alabaster'
- 2 garden rose 'Chiffon'
- 2 rose 'Quicksand'
- 3 parrot tulip 'Brownie'
- 2 lisianthus 'Alissa Brownie'
- 2 white pompom dahlias
- 3 ranunculus 'Nerone'
- 5 chocolate cosmos

METHOD

1 Scrunch up the chicken wire to create 3–4 layers that will fit inside the urn – the chicken wire should protrude from the top of the urn by 2cm (1in).

2 Secure the chicken wire in place and secure with clear pot tape in a cross overlapping the sides by approximately 1–1.5cm (½–⅝in).

3 I find it easier to make these designs in situ so if possible, move the urn to the desired location and fill with fresh, tepid water

4 Begin your design by creating the overall shape. I started with the dried cow parsley stems as they were the longest and thought their interesting shape helped start the formation of the base.

5 Next add the jasmine stems followed by the hellebores – these can be quite chunky and often flower-heavy, so consider each stem and make sure that its placement is really adding to the overall shape and design. I cut a few side shoots away from the hellebores as I felt they were too heavy – don't be afraid to do this to make them work for your design.

→

6   Once you're happy with the shape, you can start filling in using your beautiful flowers. Begin with the largest blooms – in this case, the garden roses – and work your way down to the smallest and most delicate stems – here, the cosmos.

7   Play around with placement, height and colour. It's nice to have some stems lower and deeper into the design, and some taller, or facing away. Take your time with this and don't worry if you don't get it right first time. The beauty of using chicken wire means you can easily remove the stems if you're not happy with them.

8   I finished the design with the cosmos stems to add a depth and warmth to the overall design, as well as height and a sense of movement.

TOP TIPS

As this particular arrangement was to be placed on a console table, I didn't need to consider the back of the design – but it is worth noting that if this were to be used as a table centrepiece, the design would need to look good from all angles and so more flowers and foliage would be needed.

Chrysanthemums tend to have a bit of a bad reputation but, over the years, I have come to find a new appreciation for these humble flowers, particularly the more unusual varieties. An all-time favourite is 'Vienna Copper', available from early autumn to early winter; I highly recommend getting your hands on some if you can.

AUTUMN MANTEL

WHAT YOU'LL NEED

- watertight oblong vessel that fits on your mantel (the one I used was approximately L40cm/15in, W16cm/6¼in, H16cm/6¼in)
- chicken wire
- floristry scissors

Selection of foliage and flower stems, such as:

- 5 foraged bracken stems
- 5 variegated ivy
- 3 chrysanthemum 'Vienna Copper'
- 2 chrysanthemum 'Avignon'
- 2 chrysanthemum 'Doria Salmon'
- 3 rose 'Quicksand'
- 3 panicum 'Warrior' grass
- 4 talinum 'Long John'
- 3 lisianthus 'Alessa Brownie'
- 3 parrot tulip 'Brownie'
- few stems of autumn eucalyptus

METHOD

1 Carefully scrunch the chicken wire to create 3–4 layers of wire to fit into your chosen vessel.

2 Fill the vessel three-quarters full with fresh, clean, tepid water.

3 Use the foraged bracken stems to create the shape for your design. I wanted this display to be asymmetric to complement the fireplace. Look carefully at the shape of the bracken stems you have and decide where they would work within your design to help build the shape.

4 Once you're happy, start adding the largest blooms, in this case the chrysanthemum 'Vienna Copper'. Place these at varying heights to add interest.

5 Continue to add the larger blooms making sure you don't overpower or cram the design.

6 Next, add the foliage to break up the flowers, working within the shape.

7 Finally, add the smaller stems. I love using the panicum grass and talinum 'Long John' to create height and texture.

TOP TIPS

- Take your time to build the design – enjoy choosing each stem and its placement carefully.
- Look to nature and see what you can forage to add interest to your design.

WINTER

Winter has its own unique beauty and magic like no other season. The short, crisp days and dark evenings lend themselves to relaxing at home in front of a crackling fire, while outside foliage takes on a stunning silvery-grey hue and stark branches of magnolia, birch and pussy willow provide inspiration for festive table centrepieces and winter wreaths.

While flower choice can be a little more limited, you will find ruffled ranunculus from bright white through to deep plum shades as well as elegant anemones, beautifully scented 'Paperwhite', tulips and hellebores. Winter is the perfect season to experiment with different foliage varieties, capturing the true essence of winter woodlands that are full of fragrance and glorious textures, to create a wonderful sensory experience in your home.

I absolutely love creating festive displays for friends and family to enjoy at this time of year, and when it comes to Christmas, I really do go the extra mile. After a cold, crisp winter walk, you can't beat the welcome of a hand-created door wreath followed by the beauty of a stair garland. Here you'll also find a showstopping tablescape, bringing the icy-blues and lush greens to be found outside into your dining room; a beautiful winter planter of white hyacinths to welcome in the new year; and a truly stunning hand-tied bouquet to give as a gift (or keep for yourself!).

The secret to this design is to use a wide variety of foliage and flowers in different shapes and sizes to add depth and texture. I particularly love the varying colours of the foliage, from the icy-blue eucalyptus to the lush, dark green spruce. Try foraging for interesting ingredients in your garden and in hedgerows to add to your winter table.

A WINTER TABLE

WHAT YOU'LL NEED

- watertight opaque containers,
- lengths of chicken wire
- pot tape
- floristry scissors

Selection of flowers and foliage, such as:

- 2 large Norway spruce stems
- 2 bunches ruscus
- 2 cypress branches
- 1 bunch *Eucalyptus cinerea*
- 1 bunch *Eucalyptus populus* berries
- 1 bunch *Pittosporum ralphii*
- 20 ozothamnus 'Sussex Silver'
- 20 asparagus fern stems
- 10 long ivy stems
- 1 bunch birch twigs
- 15 green eryngiums
- 20 white astrantia stems
- 1 bunch white genista
- 20 white waxflower stems

METHOD

1   Carefully concertina fold the chicken wire lengths to fit your chosen vessel to create 3–4 layers of wire.

2   Secure the chicken wire in place with pot tape, working all the way around the container and back on itself – pot tape sticks very well to itself and becomes very secure.

3   Fill your containers three-quarters-full with fresh, tepid water. I find it much easier to do this in situ as the containers can be tricky to move once filled without spilling.

4   Position your prepped containers along the length of the table and consider the shape and heigh you want to achieve – I wanted this design to capture the beauty of a winter woodland in a natural, wild and textured way without interrupting sight and conversation over dinner. It may help to sit at the table to check the design won't be too high.

5   Start placing the flower stems into the container through the spaces in the chicken wire to build a base. I started with the spruce as these were the largest stems and provided a great base and structure for the rest of the design.

    →

6   Once you've built the base continue to add one variety at a time, starting with the largest stems and finishing with the more delicate, smaller ones. Stop and stand back every now and then to check you are happy with the overall look – working this way helps you have more control over the design and ensures the height is consistent throughout the entire length.

7   Once all the foliage is in place, start inserting the flowers. I started with the white genista which effortlessly lifts the design and creates movement. I then added in the green eryngiums, which are a perfect fit for the woodland theme and add lots of texture, then the waxflower and astrantia – both beautiful filler flowers.

8   Finally, complete the design with the birch twigs – I kept these longer than everything else so that the tips poked out and added some drama.

9   Save any offcuts for the Name Place Settings (see page 170).

TOP TIPS

Before you begin, study each stems' natural shape and visualise how it will work in the design. For example, the fluffy, vibrant green asparagus fern naturally curves down so this works really well at the sides of the runner to cover the plastic containers, as well as at the ends where the runner spills over the edge of the table. The same can be said for the ivy and some of the ruscus. In contrast, the ozothamnus is long, thin, straight and pointy which lends itself perfectly to creating height when positioned down the runner at varying angles with some a little taller than the overall design.

I love to make our guests feel extra special when they're coming over for dinner, and a small posy of flowers decorating their plate or napkin is a beautiful way to welcome them to the table as well as extending your main table design (see page 164).

NAME PLACE SETTINGS

WHAT YOU'LL NEED

- offcuts and leftovers of flowers and foliage from A Winter Table (see page 164)
- floristry scissors
- thin velve ribbon

METHOD

1 Gather your offcuts and leftovers. I like to make these place settings in situ on the dressed table so I can easily get a sense of the length and size I need.
2 Lay 4–5 different stems onto a napkin in a fan shape, paying careful attention to the textures and shape you're creating.
3 Tie the flowers with ribbon in a simple bow and trim the ends of the stems to the same length. Repeat until you have a name place setting for every guest.

The winter season is not complete without a door wreath in my opinion, and making your own gives you a great excuse to get outdoors and forage for different ingredients, from pine, ivy, holly, mistletoe, yew, fir and eucalyptus. Wreath-making is so therapeutic – I highly recommend turning on the Christmas tunes and embracing the process.

TRADITIONAL WREATH

WHAT YOU'LL NEED

- 30-cm (12-in) wreath base (this could be a wire base, rattan base, or one you've created yourself from pliable branches such as clematis vine or willow)
- mossing wire or twine
- ribbon (optional)
- sphagnum moss

Selection of flowers and foliage, such as:

- 1 bundle Norway spruce
- 5 cypress branches
- 1 bunch cedar of Lebanon
- 1 bunch buxus
- ½ bunch *Eucalyptus cinerea*
- ½ bunch *Eucalyptus populus*
- 10 white waxflower stems
- 6 green eryngiums
- 10 pine cones

METHOD

1   Attach the wire or twine to the wreath base. If you're using a wire frame (as I have), it's a good idea to create a zig zag pattern with the wire or twine to make a base for the moss to sit on.

2   Add a chunky layer of moss to the wreath base and secure it by taking the wire over and under the frame the whole way around. Keep the wire attached to the wreath.

3   Cut all your foliage and flower stems to workable lengths, roughly 15–25cm (6–10in) – you want a good mixture of shapes and sizes so don't worry too much about being precise.

4   Choose the direction you would like to work around your wreath. I find it most comfortable to work in a clockwise direction as I'm right-handed, but it really doesn't matter as long as you work in the same direction the whole way around.

5   Gather a handful of your ready-trimmed foliage into a bundle in the shape of a fan.

6   Starting at the top of the wreath, position the stems of the bundle onto the middle of the moss-covered base and let the foliage fan out to cover the moss.

→

7 Attach the bundle using the wire and wrap around the ends of the stems 2-3 times until it feels secure.

8 Continue to gather and attach foliage bundles, positioning each bundle in the same direction and overlapping the previous bundle so that the wire and stems are covered. I like to choose slightly different ingredients from the previous bundle to add extra interest but try and keep the bundles roughly the same size as this will help to create an even, circular wreath.

9 When attaching the final bundle simply lift the foliage from the first bundle you created and tuck the stems of the last bundle underneath to conceal them. Wrap the wire around the final stems a few extra times to make sure it's fully secure.

10 Once all your bundles are attached, turn your wreath upside down, trim the wire at about 15–20cm (6–8in) and use it like a sewing needle looping back and forth the wire frame until it feels secure.

→

11 Use any leftover foliage to fill in any gaps or add additional texture.

12 Once all the foliage is attached, trim the green eryngiums and waxflower ends at a 45-degree angle so you have a nice point to work with and simply poke them into the wreath base. I find this gives more control over the positioning of the flowers as opposed to working them into your bundles.

13 Once you're happy with the completed design you can experiment with different ribbons to hang your wreath, or let the foliage do all the talking and simply hang the wreath with twine.

14 Generously spritz the back of the wreath directly onto the moss every 4–5 days to keep the foliage hydrated.

TOP TIPS

◆ Try to keep your workspace tidy so you can clearly see the shape of your design building. I find that with such a mass of ingredients, the surfaces are quickly covered in greenery and the wreath gets lost amongst it.

◆ Pause every so often to check you are happy with how the wreath is taking shape. I sometimes place the wreath on the floor and stand over it to get a good view. You could also ask someone to hold it up for you, or you could hold the wreath while looking at it in a mirror.

I always enjoy making winter planters on the days between Christmas and New Year for when all the decorations are packed away and the house is feeling a little bare. I have used white hyacinth bulbs here, which are readily available in garden centres at this time of year, but you could also use daffodil, muscari or amaryllis bulbs.

INDOOR WINTER PLANTER

WHAT YOU'LL NEED

- indoor watertight planter in a size and shape to suit your space (the one I used measured D43cm/20in x H16.5cm/6½in)
- gravel or pebbles
- multipurpose compost
- potted bulbs of your choice, enough to fit tightly into your chosen planter (I used 5 pots, each with 5 bulbs in). Choose bulbs that are in the early stages of growth with fresh green foliage and buds.
- moss (see page 181)

Selection of branches and twigs, such as:
- birch
- foraged lichen-covered branches
- pussy willow

METHOD

1 Water the potted bulbs well and let them sit for a couple of hours before you begin.
2 Add a 2.5cm (1in) layer of gravel or pebbles to the bottom of the planter to aid drainage and avoid waterlogging.
3 Half fill the planter with compost.
4 Carefully remove the bulbs from the pots and measure them up against the planter, adding more compost if needed. I like to see some of the actual bulbs sitting slightly higher than the rim of the planter for a natural, outdoor feel.
5 Position the bulbs in the planter and tightly pack more compost into any gaps. Hyacinth roots are particularly withstanding at this stage so you can carefully break them apart if you need to move some around without worrying about damaging them.
6 Once you're happy with the position of the bulbs, cover the compost with a layer of moss, tearing it apart to fit in between the bulbs. I'm not too neat about this as I like my planters to look wild and natural – it adds charm and reflects the outdoors.

→

7   Finally, poke the twigs and branches deep
    enough into the compost so they're nice and
    stable. Start from the middle of the planter and
    work out towards the edges. Consider the
    height that the flowers will grow to – it's likely
    the bulbs will be quite short at this stage, but
    bear in mind that hyacinths will reach around
    25cm (10in) tall and daffodils can grow as tall
    as 46cm (18in). I like to have the branches taller
    than the flowers, so they add structure and
    overall shape.
8   Position your planter in a bright spot and water
    it lightly every 2–3 days. Avoid overwatering as
    the bulbs may rot and
    won't flower.

TOP TIPS

* Once the bulbs have finished flowering,
  cut the flower stem down to the bulb
  leaving the leaves intact, then plant in
  your garden to flower next year.
* Adding in twigs and branches will help
  to support the bulbs as they grow.
  Hyacinths and daffodils tend to fall over
  under the weight of their flower heads
  – if this happens, simply prop them up
  against the branches.
* If you have moss in your garden,
  or growing on roof tiles, this can be
  used in your planter. However, you
  cannot remove moss grown in the wild
  as it is home to many beneficial micro-
  organisms and takes years to grow.

Making garlands is relatively simple, but quite time-consuming. However, they are well worth the time spent for the impact they create. I've combined foliage with a few long, trailing champagne dyed asparagus fern stems – I recommend using five or six different varieties of foliage to create lots of texture.

FOLIAGE STAIR GARLAND

WHAT YOU'LL NEED

- paper-covered wire
- bind wire .
- clear cable ties

Selection of foliage, such as:
- 1 bunch Norway spruce
- 2 bunches *Eucalyptus cinerea*
- 2 bunches *Eucalyptus Populus*
- 1 bundle cypress branches
- 2 bunches cedar of Lebanon
- 3 bunches ruscus
- 30 asparagus fern stems
- 10 champagne dyed asparagus fern stems

METHOD

1 Measure the length you'd like your finished garland to be using the paper-covered wire and cut to length. Allow for any draping, and if you're unsure cut longer than you think you'll need as it's always easier to cut it back than add to it. The paper-covered wire will hold the entire garland together – I think of it as the 'spine' of the design.

2 Attach the bind wire to the paper-covered wire by wrapping it around it a few times until secure.

3 Lay out the foliage and cut to lengths of around 20–25cm (8–10in). Don't worry too much if some are outside of this, as it's nice to have a variety.

4 Gather a handful of the ready-trimmed ingredients into a bundle in the shape of a fan. Your first bundle will be positioned at the bottom of the staircase, so consider the shape you'd like here. I wanted my garland to feel as though it was spilling out onto the floor, so my first bundle included some longer lengths of foliage such as ruscus and asparagus fern.

→

5 Attach the bundle to the paper-covered wire by wrapping the bind wire securely around the stems a few times, then leave the wire attached.

6 Continue to gather and attach bundles, laying each one on top of the previous bundle and attaching each to the paper-covered wire. Position each bundle quite close to the previous one without leaving too much of a gap as this will show once the garland is hung. I find it helpful to attach a few stems in between each of the bundles so that no part of the paper-covered wire shows.

7 Continue this process down the entire length of the paper-covered wire, ensuring the garland is building up a nice consistent shape with your desired fullness.

8 Once you reach the final bundle, attach this in the same way and when you're happy it is secure, trim the bind wire and wrap it tightly around the paper-covered wire. It will look a little messy at this stage with the stems and wire on show, but we will come back to this once it's in position.

9 Carefully carry the garland and cable ties over to your stairs. There will be a 'front' and 'back' to your garland; the back will show the wires and the front is the foliage side you've been working on. Starting at the bottom of your stairs, secure the garland to the banister by looping a cable tie through and securing, ensuring the 'front' of the garland is on show and the 'back' is hidden. Depending on the fullness of your garland, you may need two cable ties for it to be secure.

→

10 Continue up the stairs positioning and securing the garland with cable ties. I like to have a couple of drapes for a natural look, but you could keep it quite neat and tight to the banister or have more frequent drapes.

11 It's likely the garland may have a few gaps here and there, and the end where the stems are on show will need covering. Simply use some leftover foliage, trim to size and poke into the garland. To cover the end, position the foliage in the opposite direction to the rest, poking the stems into the existing final bundle. I like to use the lighter foliage for this, such as the asparagus fern and ruscus.

12 Once my garland was in position, I added the champagne dyed asparagus fern for a festive feel. I kept these subtle and placed them throughout the garland at random to avoid any symmetry or lines.

TOP TIPS

You may need an extra pair of hands to help hold the garland in place while you secure it with cable ties.

My biggest piece of advice for creating spiral hand-tied bouquets is to be relaxed, both physically and mentally. If you're feeling uptight, it will show in your bouquet – so put some calm music on, shake out any tension, and enjoy the process.

WINTER HAND-TIED BOUQUET

WHAT YOU'LL NEED

- Glass vase with tapered opening, approximately H19cm (7½in) x W19cm (7½ in)
- twine
- floristry scissors

Selection of winter flowers, such as:
- 10 daffodil 'Paperwhite'
- 10 hellebore 'Winter Bells'
- ½ bunch white genista
- 8 green eryngiums
- 8 white astrantia
- 8 white ranunculus 'White Elegance'

A variety of foliage, such as:
- 1 bunch seeded eucalyptus
- ½ bunch *Eucalyptus nicolli*
- ½ bunch *Eucalyptus cinerea*
- ½ bunch *Pittosporum ralphii*
- 6 ozomanthus

METHOD

1   Start by prepping all your ingredients by ensuring they've been well conditioned – remove all the lower foliage that would sit below the tie point and lay the stems down in front of you in groups by flower type. Spending a little time doing this means that when you're in the zone creating your bouquet, you always have the flowers easily to hand, while your other hand is busy holding the bouquet.

2   Prep your twine to tie off the bouquet – make a loop at one end of the twine and leave a length of around 7.5cm (3in) from the loop, and the other length about 20–25cm (8–10in) long (again, by prepping this beforehand, you don't need to worry about cutting and tying the string when you only have one hand spare).

3   Choose your first ingredient – I chose a large white ranunculus stem – and hold it in your non-dominant hand between your thumb, index and middle fingers.

→

4 Choose your next ingredient – I chose a stem of *Eucalyptus cinerea* – and lay it over the first stem at a slight angle, so that the stems cross over. This crossing over is the key to the bouquet naturally creating a rounded shape.

5 Turn the 2 stems a full 180 degrees – turn them over in your dominant hand and then pass them back to your non-dominant hand ready to add another stem. This will feel a bit awkward at first, but as the bouquet builds, it will become much easier. The action of adding in a stem at an angle, passing it to your other hand to turn it, and then passing it back to the original hand is the process that creates the distinctive spiral of the hand-tied bouquet.

6 Add in the next stem at the same angle you added the first and turn it in your dominant hand and pass it back to your non-dominant hand. Hold the stems loosely – it doesn't matter at this stage if they drop down a little as you can easily pull them back up.

7 Continue adding stems and turning the bouquet until you've used all the ingredients. As the bouquet builds, you will find it becomes much easier to add stems and turn the bouquet, and the stems will form a beautiful spiral. How far you turn the bouquet each time is likely to vary as you notice gaps, and places you want your flowers and foliage to sit.

→

8   Once you're happy with your design, take the length of twine you prepped at the beginning and hook the loop over the little finger of the hand that's holding the bouquet. Wrap the longer length around the bouquet and take it through the loop. Pull the length of twine back on itself and go around again to meet the other length of twine and tie a knot that's tight and secure.

9   Measure the bouquet against your chosen vase and trim the ends of your stems over a bin using sharp, clean floristry scissors, if needed. Remember that it's always better to leave the stems too long and be able to cut more off later, rather than to have taken too much off. Ideally you want the lowest flowers of the bouquet to touch the rim of the vase. The stems are too long if the bouquet tilts to one side of the vase.

TOP TIPS

• Don't worry if your bouquet isn't exactly as you imagined; this is a tricky design to master, but once you've 'got it', you won't be able to stop making these!

• Most winter flowers have shorter stem lengths of around 30–40cm (12–16in), so it's important to consider the vase you choose for this design carefully. A glass vase will show off the spiralling stems perfectly.

A mantlepiece provides a wonderful focal point and is the perfect architectural structure to cover in an abundance of fragrant and festive foliage. Just remember that if your mantlepiece sits above a heat source, you'll need to water your arrangement to ensure it lasts. You can easily water the moss regularly with a long-spouted watering can.

FOLIAGE MANTLE ARRANGEMENT

WHAT YOU'LL NEED

- watertight plastic tray, appropriately sized for your mantle
- chicken wire
- pot tape
- floristry scissors
- sphagnum moss

Selection of foliage, such as:
- 3 bunches ruscus (approximately 115cm/45in long)
- 1 bunch seeded eucalyptus
- 1 bunch acacia
- 1 bunch *Eucalyptus populus*
- 1 bunch *Pittosporum ralphii*
- 1 bunch *Eucalyptus cinerea*
- 1 bunch *Eucalyptus nicolli*
- 20 asparagus fern stems

METHOD

1 Start by creating the mossed tray mechanic. Carefully cut the chicken wire to the same length as the tray, and a little more than double its width.

2 Place a layer of moss in the bottom of the tray.

3 Fold the chicken wire down the middle lengthways to create a V shape. Start packing the moss into the folded chicken wire. As the moss builds, start to bring the ends of the chicken wire together, keeping one side flat and the other more rounded to create a tunnel shape. Ensure the moss is well packed – you don't want it to be so tight that you can't insert enough stems, but equally, you don't want it too loose, so the stems aren't held securely.

4 Position the flat side of the chicken wire tunnel onto the tray and then secure in place along the tray with pot tape. Pot tape sticks best to itself, so take it all the way under and over the tray. (I did this 3 times, middle and ends, but you may need less or more, depending on the length of the tray, until it's secure.)

5 If the moss is a little dry, give it a generous spritz with water until damp.

→

6   Position the mossed tray in the middle of your mantle. Before you start adding the foliage, consider the shape you're going to create. I wanted this design to be quite wild and natural, so I avoided any obvious symmetry and kept one side taller and long, and the other end low and long.

7   Start by using the long ruscus stems to create the shape. Cut each stem at a sharp angle (this will make it easier to insert into the moss) and insert them into the moss by approximately 5cm (2in) to anchor them into position – I used 8 stems to create the overall shape. Ruscus is a great option as it can easily be moulded into shape by gently bending it into a position you're happy with. Stand back from the design and study the shape you've created and make any necessary tweaks.

8   Once you're happy with the shape, add in your other stems, following the shape you've created while paying close attention to the length and position. It's good to use a variety of lengths to build up depth and texture but try not to lose your overall shape in doing so. Use your next largest stems and work your way down to the smallest and most delicate. Here, the order I used my ingredients was, ruscus, *Eucalyptus cinerea*, seeded eucalyptus, acacia, *Eucalyptus populus*, *Pittosporum ralphii*, *Eucalyptus nicholii*, asparagus fern.

9   Lightly spritz or water the moss base with a long-spouted watering can every other day.

TOP TIPS

When I'm in the throes of working on larger designs, I like to walk out of the room and distract myself with doing something else for a few minutes. I'll then re-entrer the room with fresh eyes and I find I notice things I otherwise may have overlooked – whether it's a small gap that needs filling, or that the scale has got too large.

CREATING YOUR OWN ARRANGEMENTS

I think it's important to define what an arrangement actually means. To some, it means a large, impressive floral display that takes skill, expertise and know-how to create. To others, it can portray complicated, intricate and often intimidating designs that only belong in books and extravagant events. The truth is, a floral arrangement is a 'decorative arrangement of flowers'. That's it. No rules or regulations on the types of flowers, the technique or the size. Just something that you want to create and that you believe looks visually pleasing.

For the projects in this book, I created a wide span of differing arrangements, from petite name place settings, small bedside bowl arrangements through to large draping stair garlands and elaborate mantel designs in our home. I hope there is an arrangement here for you, one that has got your creative juices flowing, and perhaps something you can put your own spin and unique stamp on. If you desire, you can of course create the exact arrangements exactly as I have in this book, but for me, it's not about that. Of course, using the same techniques will support you and give you confidence in arranging, but I would encourage you to take the time to develop your own style and make the arrangements unique to you.

Whether you decide to create an elaborate Christmas mantel over the festive period for your family and friends to admire, or a beautiful seasonal door wreath to celebrate the arrival of spring, I hope I've inspired you to explore flowers in new ways you hadn't previously considered.

This book, my first, holds a lot of information, and I truly hope it's a useful resource and inspiring read. But, above all, I hope you find joy in flowers and feel confident and excited that you have the right tools and skills to continue your floral journey and harness the beauty that each season has to offer within your homes.

FLOWER DIRECTORY

Here you will find a comprehensive guide to my most-loved stems throughout the seasons. To help you plan for floral designs, I have grouped them by their seasons and split into three categories; Focal Flowers, Supporting Flowers and Filler Flowers, which you can read more about in the Selecting Your Flowers section (see page 20). You may notice that some flowers feature across multiple seasons due to their longevity, and some flowers may feature in more than one category within the same season; depending on the way you use them in your designs, they could lend themselves to multiple categories.

SPRING FLOWERS

FOCAL FLOWERS
—

Botanical name: *Allium*
Common name: Ornamental Onion
Attributes: Most varieties have a distinct large spherical flower head on long straight stems, often referred to as 'lollipops', or 'pom-poms'. Available in white and shades of purple, we have many of these in our garden where they make beautiful pops of colour in spring, but I also love to work a few into my spring arrangements as focal flowers.
Scent: As the common name suggests, these exude an oniony scent.

Botanical name: *Anemone*
Common name: Windflower
Attributes: A simple pretty flower with large, rounded petals and distinctive dark centres. Available in a variety of colours from bright white through to deep burgundy. On arrival, the petals may be tightly closed, but they will open in response to light and warmth to reveal their beauty.
Scent: None

Botanical name: *Fritillaria persica*
Common name: Persian Lily
Attributes: Tall stems (one of the tallest for spring) with greyish-green slender foliage and sumptuous towering, nodding bell-shaped deep plum flowers.
Scent: Musky

Botanical name: *Helleborus*
Common name: Hellebore
Attributes: Delicate cupped flower heads that naturally bow down available in muted greens, pure white,

pale pinks and deep maroons. I love the double varieties with an abundance of petals, making them a perfect focal flower for winter and spring arrangements. See Flower Conditioning on page 24 for how to care for these flowers.
Scent: None

Botanical name: *Hyacinthus*
Common name: Hyacinth
Attributes: Densely packed with small star-shaped flowers and long, vibrant, green leaves on thick, soft stems. Available in a variety of colours, my favourites being white, pale pink and purple.
Scent: Highly fragrant with a sweet scent that can easily fill a room.

Botanical name: *Narcissus*
Common name: Daffodil
Attributes: Thin long stems with single flowers with a central trumpet- shaped crown with frilled edges. Well-known for its vibrant yellow varieties, but I love some of the more interesting colours like 'Pink Charm' with its peachy trumpet and delicate white petals, 'Watch Up' with white petals and an extremely pale-yellow trumpet and 'My Story', with ruched and curvy petals in white and peach. I also can't resist the scent and delicacy of 'Paperwhite' during winter and spring with multiple small flowers per stem.
Scent: Sweet

Botanical name: *Ranunculus*
Common name: Buttercup
Attributes: Its name, ranunculus, means 'little frog' as these bulbous

flowers were first discovered growing along streams during spring. A beautiful and ruffled flower with tissue-thin petals available in a huge range of colours during winter and spring. My favourite varieties include 'Hanoi', a chunky yet, soft and romantic pale pink, as well as 'Nerone Extreme', a deep, dark burgundy. The 'Butterfly' varieties are extremely pretty and delicate with multiple flowers and buds. If you love peonies but can't wait for them to arrive, then ranunculus are the perfect spring alternative.
Scent: Sweet

Botanical name: *Syringa*
Common name: Lilac
Attributes: Large cone-shaped blooms comprising clusters of small and delicate flowers make this a highly textured flower to add to your arrangements. They're not around for long, just a few short weeks in spring, and if you're lucky enough to have a lilac tree in your garden, you can snip a few branches to enjoy inside. lilac is a woody stem; see Flower Conditioning on page 24 for how to care for these flowers. Lilac has large lush green leaves and I recommend removing these to allow the water to concentrate its effort on the flower heads. Available in white, pale lilac and lavender.
Scent: Light and sweet fragrance.

Botanical name: *Tulipa*
Common name: Tulip
Attributes: These popular flowers can be found almost anywhere during spring, but my favourites are the double and parrot varieties with

an abundance of blousy petals and streaks of varying colours. Tulips tend to naturally droop due to their soft stems and heavy flower heads and they will move around in response to light and warmth which is magical to watch. However, if you prefer your stems to be straighter, as soon as you get them wrap them securely in brown paper, snip the ends, and allow them to rest and drink fresh water for 24 hours. When you remove the paper, they will have straightened out.
Scent: Varying from none, to fresh and citrusy.

SUPPORTING FLOWERS
—

Botanical name: *Clematis*
Common name: Clematis
Attributes: Star-shaped flowers with long petals and thin, hard stems with attractive green foliage. Available in an array of beautiful purple tones as well as white and pink. I love using these elegant stems to create shape, height and interest. *Clematis Old Mans beard* can be found in hedgerows and bought as a cut flower and, as it's name suggests, it has small hairy white flower heads that add lots of great interest in autumn.
Scent: Very light fragrance

Botanical name: *Genista*
Common name: Broom
Attributes: An upright branch with an abundance of slender stems and petite flowers that cluster together along the stems, available in white, pinks, peaches and yellow. This stem adds plenty of texture and movement thanks to the abundance of stems and small flowers.
Scent: Beautiful, sweet fragrance – my spring favourite.

Botanical name: *Magnolia*
Common name: Magnolia
Attributes: Whether their flower heads are still small fluffy buds, just peeping open, or even fully in bloom, magnolia branches are a stunning addition to your arrangements that reflect spring's beauty. These are thirsty, woody stems (see Flower Conditioning on page 24 for how to care for these flowers) so keep the water topped up.

Scent: None as buds, light and sweet when in bloom.

Botanical name: *Salix matsudana*
Common name: Contorted/Curly Willow
Attributes: Gracefully curly and twisted bare branches that I use in a variety of designs such as spring planters, to add height and support for tall blooms, and hand-tied bouquets, to create shape and interest.
Scent: None

Botanical name: *Spiraea*
Common name: Meadowsweet
Attributes: Magical, tall, arching branches with delicate clusters of white flowers that are brilliant for creating a shape and structure for your arrangements, while adding softness and elegance.
Scent: None

Botanical name: *Viburnum opulus*
Common name: Guelder Rose
Attributes: Snowball-shaped green flower heads made up of clusters of tiny petals that appear as though they bounce on the ends of leafy branched stems. They have woody stems, which can make them prone to wilting (see Flower Conditioning on page 24 for how to care for these flowers) but in my opinion, they are well worth a little extra care for the bountiful zingy blooms that effortlessly lift an arrangement and add so much life and volume. These stems benefit from some flower food, plenty of clean water and being kept out of direct sunlight, or warm spots.
Scent: None

FILLER FLOWERS
—

Botanical name: *Fritillaria meleagris*
Common name: Checkered Lily
Attributes: Beautifully delicate bowing flower heads with long slender leaves. Its distinctive pattern is reminiscent of a snake's skin, and I love the deep purple colour for spring arrangements. Like tulips, they have a tendency to bend, making them ideal to place over the edge of bowls or rims of vases.
Scent: None

Botanical name: *Genista 'Repetition'*
Common name: Broom
Attributes: An upright branch with an abundance of slender stems and petite flowers that cluster together along the stems, available in white, pinks, peaches and yellow. This stem adds plenty of texture and movement.
Scent: Beautiful, sweet fragrance – my spring favourite.

Botanical name: *Leucojum aestivum*
Common name: Summer Snowflake
Attributes: Delicate and petite stems with multiple bell-shaped white flowers with small green marks on each petal, as though someone has hand-painted them on. Their short stem length and natural curve means that they lend themselves beautifully to the edges of arrangements.

SUMMER FLOWERS

FOCAL FLOWERS
—

Botanical name: *Dahlia*
Common name: Dahlia
Attributes: From densely packed pom-poms, to wide, exquisite 'dinner plate' varieties, dahlias come into season in mid-summer through to the first frosts. The flowers come in a vast array of colours, shapes and sizes and the blooms are front-facing as opposed to upright, so work beautifully on the sides of arrangements. Their vase life is shorter than most at around five days. My favourite varieties are; 'Café au Lait', 'Jowey Winnie', 'Labryinth' and 'Sweet Nathalie'. They're great to add to your garden borders or pots.
Scent: None

Botanical name: *Delphinium*
Common name: Delphinium
Attributes: Tall flower spikes with clusters of open blooms all the way to the top of the stem. Ideal for creating height in your arrangements – I like to vary the size and angle of them in my designs to give balance and a natural feel. Most commonly available in white, blue and purple.
Scent: None

Botanical name: *Digitalis*
Common name: Foxglove
Attributes: Large flat leaves at the base of the stem with tall, upright flower spikes with distinctive bell-shaped flowers that stretch to the top of the spike. Available in white, purple and peach tones. Always handle with gloves as they are poisonous.
Scent: None

Botanical name: *Hydrangea*
Common name: Hydrangea
Attributes: See page 201.
Scent: None

Botanical name: *Paeonia*
Common name: Peony
Attributes: Starting off as tightly enclosed buds, the flowers develop with petals that initially curve inward to form bowl-like centres before they put on the real show and open up to become huge ruffled blooms. Long stems with a generous amount of attractive lush, green foliage. Available in white, pink, coral, red, purple. My favourite varieties include; 'Bowl of Cream', 'Mother's Choice', 'Dinner Plate' and 'Coral Sunset'.
Scent: Light sweet or citrusy fragrance

Botanical name: *Rosa*
Common name: Rose
Attributes: The most popular flower in the world and with its vast array of colour, shape and size it's easy to see why. My favourite roses are created by David Austin – 'Leonora' and 'Patience' are my favourite ivory roses and 'Kiera' is an incredibly beautiful soft pink. The scent is exquisite – I wish I could bottle it up. Allow your roses plenty of time (sometimes up to five days) and space to open up, ensuring their well-conditioned.
Scent: Dependent on variety.

Botanical name: *Scabiosa*
Common name: Pincushion
Attributes: Long slender stems with simplistic swathes of foliage and delicate flower heads that appear to dance on the end of their stems. Often referred to as 'pincushions' thanks to their intricately detailed and prominent stamen in the centre of each bloom. Available in plenty of colours, my favourites are whites, pale pinks and deep burgundy shades.
Scent: None

SUPPORTING FLOWERS
—

Botanical name: *Ammi majus*
Common name: Bishop's Flower
Attributes: Tall pale green stems with delicate, airy white domed flower heads reminiscent of lace-work, with wispy foliage. These soft, frothy blooms make beautiful supporting and filler flowers.
Scent: None

Botanical name: *Antirrhinum*
Common name: Snapdragon
Attributes: Tall flower spikes with symmetrical ruffled petals reminiscent of a closed lip-like mouth that bloom from the bottom of the spike first. Available in many colours from pastel peaches and pinks to vibrant orange, yellow, white and even two-toned varieties. Their tall spikes are perfect for creating height and shape in your designs.
Scent: None

Botanical name: *Astilbe*
Common name: Goat's Beard
Attributes: Beautifully elegant and fluffy upright flower plumes on dark green leafy foliage on thin stems. Available in white, pink, red and purple tones. Ideal as both an attractive filler and supporting stem to create height and shape.
Scent: None

Botanical name: *Campanula*
Common name: Bellflower
Attributes: Tubular bell-shaped flowers loosely clustered up the length of this beautiful upright flower stem. Available in white, blue, purple and pink, ideal for creating height and shape in your arrangements.
Scent: None

Botanical name: *Eustoma*
Common name: Lisianthus
Attributes: Available as single or double varieties. The doubles, when allowed time to fully bloom, can be reminiscent of soft, romantic roses. The tall stems with multiple branches and a generous amount of flowers and buds that work beautifully as a supporting flower to create height, shape and interest.
Scent: None

Botanical name: *Matthiola*
Common name: Stock
Attributes: Tall flower spikes with densely packed showy flowers up the length of the stem. Available in a wide variety of colours from white, pale pinks and lavender as well as deeper jewel tones of purple, pink and red. Their spiked shape makes them ideal as a supporting flower to create height, shape and interest.
Scent: Highly fragrant sweet scent.

Botanical name: *Scabiosa*
Common name: Scabious
Attributes: See left.
Scent: None

FILLER FLOWERS
—

Botanical name: *Ammi majus*
Common name: Bishop's Flower
Attributes: See page left.
Scent: None

Botanical name: *Anthriscus sylvestris*
Common name: Cow Parsley
Attributes: From spring to early summer, cow parsley turns hedgerows into tall, frothy white borders that dance in the breeze with their umbrella-like white clusters of flowers. It is a wonderful stem to forage and add to your arrangements for a wild, soft and natural element.
Scent: Light parsley fragrance

Botanical name: *Astrantia*
Common name: Masterwort
Attributes: Star shaped flowers with intricate detail available in white and shades of purple. Each stem has multiple flowers making them a great filler flower and their delicacy adds a softness to your designs to break up large focal flowers.
Scent: Musky

Botanical name: *Astilbe*
Common name: Goat's Beard
Attributes: See page 202.
Scent: None

Botanical name: *Cosmos bipinnatua*
Common name: Cosmos
Attributes: Daisy-like flowers with large delicate petals on long slender stems with wispy foliage. My favourite varieties are; 'Purity' – a saucer-shaped bright white flower, 'Cupcake Blush' – with delicate pleated petals in soft pink, 'Apricot Lemonande' – one of the newest varieties with a unique colour of soft apricot with a dusty lavender reverse, and 'Chocolate' – a petite flower with dark and moody maroon petals. These are fabulously rewarding flowers to grow in your garden as they continue to bloom the more they are cut, and they add delicacy and lightness to your arrangements.
Scent: Varying dependent on the variety.

Botanical name: *Lathyrus*
Common name: Sweet Peas
Attributes: Straight thin stems grown on climbing vines with a powerful, beautiful fragrance. Available in a huge array of colours with romantic, curving petals that effortlessly add prettiness and delicacy to your designs. The vines also make for interesting foliage to add to your designs with their twisting stems and green leaves.
Scent: Highly fragrant, reminiscent of rose and orange blossom.

Botanical name: *Nigella*
Common name: Love-in-a-mist
Attributes: Pretty and delicate tall stems with fine spindly foliage and petite flowers available in white, purple and blue and with distinctive seed pods. If you're growing these in your garden, keep cutting them to encourage more flowers, but leave a few on to use the beautiful seed pods for late summer and autumn flowering interest.
Scent: None

Botanical name: *Orlaya grandiflora*
Common name: White Laceflower
Attributes: Delicate and extremely pretty umbellifer white flower heads on tall thin stems adding softness and romance to your designs.
Scent: None

Botanical name: *Clematis*
Common name: Clematis
Attributes: See page 201.
Scent: Very light fragrance

AUTUMN FLOWERS

FOCAL FLOWERS
—

Botanical name: *Dahlias*
Common name: Dahlias
Attributes: See page 201.
Scent: None

Botanical name: *Chrysanthemum*
Common name: Mum or Chrysanth
Attributes: Generally speaking, chrysanthemums have had a poor reputation amongst florists and flower lovers, but over the last few years, they have made a big comeback thanks to original and quirky varieties in fabulous colour ways that are perfect for autumn. They are a great alternative to dahlias and have an impressive vase life. Some of my favourites are 'Spider Bronze' and 'Tula Purple', the flower form of a firework with long spiky petals and soft warm colour tones. 'Bigoudi Red', a deep, rich, red with beautiful unfurling petals. 'Avignon Pink', a great substitute to the 'Café au Lait' dahlia with soft apricot tones, and 'Vienna Copper', a fabulously pink and copper- toned flower with long slender petals that curve inwards and slowly unfurl to reveal their beauty.
Scent: Earthy

Botanical name: *Hydrangea*
Common name: Hydrangea
Attributes: Available throughout the whole year, but at their peak from mid-summer to autumn. I love pure white and green varieties, and deep plum colours in autumn, but you can get hold of these in a huge array of colours from blue, pink, red and purple. They have woody stems, so they do need a little extra care to slit up the length of the stems (see flower conditioning, woody stems, for full details) to maximise their water intake. Hydrangea also drink from their petals and leaves so they will enjoy a generous misting.
Scent: None

SUPPORTING FLOWERS
—

Botanical name: *Anemone hupehensis*
Common name: Japanese Anemone
Attributes: Tall stems with an abundance of saucer shaped flowers and pretty buds on each stem. Available in soft pinks, deep purple and white, they're a great way of adding Autumnal structure, delicacy and interest to your designs.
Scent: None

Botanical name: *Crocosmia*
Common name: Falling Stars
Attributes: Crocosmia seed heads are a tall straight stem with beautiful interest and colour as the flowers form seed pods. Ideal for adding height, shape and interest.
Scent: None

Botanical name: *Erynigium*
Common name: Sea Holly
Attributes: Eryngiums are ornamental thistles available in deep blue and pale green colour tones and are ideal for adding texture and depth to your designs.
Scent: None

Botanical name: *Skimmia*
Common name: Skimmia
Attributes: Cone shaped heads with tightly packed buds with large, green leathery leaves. Available in red and green – they add beautiful interest and depth to your designs.
Scent: Earthy

FILLER FLOWERS
—

Botanical name: *Clematis*
Common name: Clematis
Attributes: See page 201.
Scent: Very light fragrance.

Botanical name: *Sanguisorba*
Common name: Burnet
Attributes: Branched wiry stems with small deep red flower bobbles that appear to dance around creating airy movement to your designs.
Scent: None

Botanical name: *Talinum paniculatum*
Common name: 'Long John'
Attributes: Wispy yet structural tall stem with small and delicate red-brown berry-like flowers. This is a beautiful filler to add plenty of interest and depth to your designs.
Scent: None

WINTER FLOWERS

FOCAL FLOWERS
—

Botanical name: *Amaryllis*
Common name: Amaryllis
Attributes: Large trumpet shaped flowers on tall hollow stems, most commonly seen in white and red. However, varieties also include soft pinks, apricot and peaches and deep red. Each stem contains multiple flower heads making them a large and showy flower to use in your Winter arrangements.
Scent: Sweet and delicate.

Botanical name: *Anemone*
Common name: Windflower
Attributes: See page 200.
Scent: None

Botanical name: *Helleborus*
Common name: Hellebore
Attributes: See page 200.
Scent: None

Botanical name: *Hyacinthus*
Common name: Hyacinth
Attributes: See page 200.
Scent: Highly fragrant with a sweet scent that can easily fill a room.

Botanical name: *Narcissus*
Common name: Daffodils
Attributes: See page 200.
Scent: Sweet

Botanical name: *Ranunculus*
Common name: Buttercup
Attributes: See page 200.
Scent: Sweet

Botanical name: *Tulipa*
Common name: Tulip
Attributes: See page 200.
Scent: Varying from none, to fresh and citrusy.

SUPPORTING FLOWERS
—

Botanical name: *Narcissus*
Common name: Daffodils
Attributes: See page 200.
Scent: Sweet

Botanical name: *Tulipa*
Common name: Tulip
Attributes: See page 200.
Scent: Varying from none, to fresh and citrusy.

FILLER FLOWERS
—

Botanical name: *Astrantia*
Common name: Masterwort
Attributes: Star-shaped flowers with intricate detail available in white and shades of purple. Each stem has multiple flowers making them a great filler flower and their delicacy adds a softness to your designs to break up large focal flowers.
Scent: Musky

Botanical name: *Chamelaucium*
Common name: Waxflower
Attributes: Long thin woody branches with multiple side stems, short straight foliage, and a generous scattering of small and pretty flowers. Available in white or shades of pink. Ideal as a long lasting filler flower for adding texture and delicacy.
Scent: Rich honey-lemon

Botanical name: *Skimmia*
Common name: Skimmia
Attributes: Cone shaped heads with tightly packed buds with large, green leathery leaves. Available in red and green – they add beautiful interest and depth to your designs.
Scent: Earthy

INDEX

ACKNOWLEDGEMENTS

It never crossed my mind that my name would grace the front cover of a book as an author, but here we are, and what an incredible journey it has been! Philippa, Commissioning Editor at Greenfinch, thank you for reaching out and asking if I'd be interested in writing this book. I could hardly believe it when your email landed in my inbox – thank you for seeing something in me. Without you, this book simply would not exist. To Helena, our incredibly talented photographer, thank you for capturing the flowers so beautifully and taking photos of me that I don't actually mind! To Sarah, art director and styling queen. I will never be able to style pears in a bowl as well as you! Thank you for making our shoots so enjoyable and for completely putting me at ease. I will treasure the memories we made on those flower-filled days, even if we did almost flood the lounge and very nearly set the Christmas garland on fire! You are both wonderful, kind and very talented women.

Mum and Dad, an enormous thank you for always being there to help and support in any way possible, from bringing us food when we didn't have the time to cook, to looking after our girls. Nothing was ever too much. I love you so much, thank you for your patience, love, and support. To Chris, my wonderful husband. Special thanks for your unwavering support and for believing in me every single step of the way. I am forever grateful that you never once questioned the number of times we had to take the TV off the wall, wash out the floristry buckets, and for knowing exactly when I needed a coffee or can of cola! Thank you for the hours you've devoted, over many evenings and weekends, in between running our own business, to help me to meticulously plan the projects. I love you and I can't imagine my life without you. Orla and Florence, my beautiful girls, aged just two and three at the time of writing this book. Your purity and innocence have kept me grounded, thank you for being a constant reminder of what's important in life. The image of you both twirling around with flower crowns on your heads being princesses is one I'll treasure forever. I look forward to the day I can sit down with you both and enjoy showing you this book. I love you more than you'll ever know.

First published in Great Britain in 2023 by Greenfinch
An imprint of Quercus Editions Ltd
Carmelite House
50 Victoria Embankment
London
EC4Y 0DZ

An Hachette UK company
Copyright © Ashlee Jane 2023

The moral right of Ashlee Jane to be identified as the author of this work has been asserted in accordance with the Copyright, Designs and Patents Act, 1988.

A CIP catalogue record for this book is available from the British Library.

HB ISBN 978-152942-118-7
eBook ISBN 978-1-52942-119-4

Quercus Editions Ltd hereby exclude all liability to the extent permitted by law for any errors or omissions in this book and for any loss, damage or expense (whether direct or indirect) suffered by a third party relying on any information contained in this book.

10 9 8 7 6 5 4 3 2 1

Design by Sarah Pyke
Photography by Helena Dolby

Printed and bound in China
Papers used by Greenfinch are from well-managed forests and other responsible sources.